Thomas Schirrmacher (Ed.)

William Carey: Theologian – Linguist – Social Reformer

"World of Theology Series"

Studies published by the Theological Commission of the World Evangelical Alliance

Vol 4

Vol 1 Thomas K. Johnson: The First Step in Missions Training: How our Neighbors are Wrestling with God's General Revelation
Vol 2 Thomas K. Johnson: Christian Ethics in Secular Cultures
Vol 3 David Parker: Discerning the Obedience of Faith: A Short History of the World Evangelical Alliance Theological Commission
Vol 4 Thomas Schirrmacher (Ed.): William Carey: Theologian – Linguist – Social Reformer
Vol 5 Thomas Schirrmacher: Advocate of Love – Martin Bucer as Theologian and Pastor
Vol 6 Thomas Schirrmacher: Culture of Shame / Culture of Guilt
Vol 7 Thomas Schirrmacher: The Koran and the Bible
Vol 8 Thomas Schirrmacher (Ed.): The Humanisation of Slavery in the Old Testament
Vol 9 Jim Harries: New Foundations for Appreciating Africa: Beyond Religious and Secular Deceptions
Vol 10 Thomas Schirrmacher: Missio Dei – God's Missional Nature
Vol 11 Thomas Schirrmacher: Biblical Foundations for 21st Century World Mission

Thomas Schirrmacher (Ed.)

William Carey: Theologian – Linguist – Social Reformer

Essays from four continents

by Terry G. Carter, P. Sam Daniel,
George Ella, C. P. Hallihan,
Vishal Mangalwadi, Bruce J. Nicholls,
Thomas Schirrmacher

WIPF & STOCK · Eugene, Oregon

Wipf and Stock Publishers
199 W 8th Ave, Suite 3
Eugene, OR 97401

William Carey
Theologian, Linguist, Social Reformer
By Schirrmacher, Thomas
Copyright©2013 Verlag für Kultur und Wissenschaft
ISBN 13: 978-1-5326-5526-5
Publication date 4/10/2018
Previously published by Verlag für Kultur und Wissenschaft, 2013

"... If once God would by his Spirit convince of Sin, a Saviour would be a blessing indeed to them; but Human Nature is the very same all the world over; and all Conviction fails except it is produced by the effectual working of the Holy Spirit."

William Carey reporting on a discussion with a money-changer in his Journal, February 1, 1794[1]

"You and I, and all of us are Sinners, and we are in a helpless state but I have good things to tell you. God in the riches of his Mercy became incarnate, in the form of Man. He lived more than thirty years on the earth but without Sin and was employed in doing good. He gave sight to the Blind, healed the Sick, the Lame, the Deaf and the Dumb – and after all died in the stead of Sinners. We deserved the wrath of God, but he endured it. We could make no sufficient atonement for our guilt but he completely made an end of Sin and now he has sent us to tell you that the Work is done and to call you to faith in, and dependence on the Lord Jesus Christ. Therefore, leave your vain customs, and false gods, and lay hold of eternal Life through him."

William Carey in a Letter to Andrew Fuller about the conversion of a Hindu in November, 1800[2]

---

[1] Terry G. Carter. The Journal and Selected Letters of William Carey. Macon (GA): Smyth & Helwys, 2000, p. 15. The quotes were selected by Dr Carter for this volume.

[2] Ibid., p. 149.

Contents

THOMAS K. JOHNSON: Foreword:
The Holistic Mission of William Carey 9

TERRY G. CARTER: The Calvinism of William Carey
And Its Effect on His Mission Work 13
    Introduction 13
    The Calvinism of William Carey the Missionary 24
    Conclusion 33
    Bibliography 34

SAM DANIEL: William Carey's Contribution to Indian Languages 37
    1. William Carey (1761-1834) 37
    2. Protestant Missionary Assumptions Regarding Language Use 37
    3. The Translation Strategy Adopted by Carey 38
    4. Carey's Contribution to Bengali 39
    5. To Conclude 41
    References 42

GEORGE ELLA: William Carey: Using God's Means to Convert the
People of India 43
    Part One: How Carey Became a Missionary 43
    Part Two: Early Pioneer Work 51
    Part Three: Harvesting at Serampore 58
    Part Four: The Serampore Trio Triumph over Opposition from the
        Home Front 66

C. P. HALLIHAN: William Carey
"A plodder for Christ", "Father of modern Missions", but,
mostly, Bible Translator 75
    Introduction 75
    Profile: beginnings 76
    Profile: the sending 77
    Mission and the Bible 78
    Carey's Bibles 79
    Bible Societies 81
    Conclusion 82

VISHAL MANGALWADI: India: Perils and Promise Then And Now 85
    Human Waste Then 86
    Changing India for the Better 89
    William Carey's efforts 91
    Does the 21st Century Need Reformers? 94

BRUCE J. NICHOLLS: The Theology of William Carey 97
    Biblical Foundations 98
    Christology for Mission 99
    The Gathered Church 100
    Faith and Culture 103
    Integral Mission 106

THOMAS SCHIRRMACHER: Be keen to get going 109
    1. Carey's Theology – the 'Missing Link' 109
    2.1 Postmillennialism and Missions 114
    2.2. Carey's Postmillennialism 135
    3. Carey's Calvinism 141
    4. Carey's Statistics 152

Foreword: The Holistic Mission of William Carey

By Thomas K. Johnson, Ph.D.

Johnson has served as the pastor of three evangelical churches and taught philosophy or theology in ten universities and theological schools in nine countries. He is currently Vice President for Research for Martin Bucer Seminary (Germany, Austria, Switzerland, Czech Republic, Turkey, and Brazil), Adjunct Professor of Social Studies at Vilnius Pedagogical University (Lithuania), Professor of Theology, Philosophy and Public Policy for the International Institute for Christian Studies, and Director of the Comenius Institute (Prague, Czech Republic).

By publishing this book we are obviously suggesting that William Cary and his team, though not without weaknesses, are worthy role models for Christians. This does not mean they were sinless or faultless. Like normal people, they caused many of their own problems. Nor does it mean that missionaries today should imitate Carey in a wooden manner. Wise mission strategy always requires a living assessment of the needs of people in a particular situation and also of the talents which God has given to particular members of the body of Christ. (See the obviously connected parables of Jesus in Matthew 25:14-46 about applying talents to needs.)[3] But there are noteworthy patterns in the mission efforts of Carey's team that are instructive in a manner that goes beyond encouraging us to imitate their courage, endurance, love, and creativity. These patterns were inseparable from the way in which they both led many people to faith in Christ and also brought significant directional changes in Indian society.

I. Carey's team applied the biblical message to many different dimensions of life and culture.

Of course Carey and his colleagues preached the gospel to individuals and organized the converts into churches. But because of the organic holism

---

[3] I am thinking here of the three aspects of all decision making which Thomas Schirrmacher and John Frame have explained in various contexts. These are the normative, the situational, and existential aspects. Somewhat simplified, for missions the Great Commission is the norm; an assessment of a particular people group to which missionaries are sent provides the situation; and the talents given by God to these particular missionaries are central to the existential aspect of mission decisions.

they perceived in the biblical message, they also became leaders in primary and higher education; in agriculture; in business; in stabilizing multiple languages and putting them into writing; in translating, editing, and publishing the Bible and many other books (including Indian classics); and in reforming the civil laws into something that was much more humane. Many came to faith in Christ. And through their holistic missionary efforts, there was a change of direction in the most diverse areas of Indian culture that helped many more, even millions who did not come to faith in Jesus. Written languages as well as laws prohibiting widow burning, infanticide, and human trafficking were gifts of God's common grace, given by God through sacrificial missionary efforts, while the priceless gift of knowing salvation in Jesus was the gift of God's special grace to all who believed the gospel. The example set by Carey's team reminds me of the instructions of the prophet Jeremiah to the Israelites carried into captivity in Babylon: "Seek the peace and prosperity of the city to which I have carried you into exile." (Jeremiah 29:7) The group of missionaries with Carey made some significant strides toward bringing peace and prosperity to India.

II. Carey's team maintained a dynamic complementarity in their theology which should guide missions.

William Carey was a gloomy Calvinist when it came to describing human nature. He talked freely of the total depravity[4] of the human heart and the way in which sin influences all of human customs and literature. He believed many of the established customs of his day were the result of total depravity, customs such as the caste system, slavery, throwing one's children into a river to attain purity, polygamy, or the marriage of small girls to older men, so that many were widows by the age of four. On the other hand, like many of the Calvinists of his era, he also believed that there are aspects of the kingdom of God that can become present in our time by means of the preaching, teaching, and application of God's Word. In this sense, Carey was a very serious optimist and believed that many evils in the world could be stopped and replaced by much better customs and practices. He thought that under the influence of God's Word, the earthly future of the human race could be much better than the past. This dynamic complementarity in theology was central to the missionary vigor of their group, so that they were always on the edge of pessimism about human nature but

---

[4] When Calvinists talk about total depravity they usually mean that sin and depravity influence the totality of human life, not that all people are as bad as they can possibly be.

optimism about the presence of God's kingdom, without naïveté but filled with godly hope.

III. Carey's team used appropriately diverse methods for relating the biblical message to cultures.

Carey and his colleagues related the biblical message to their cultural situation in multiple and complementary ways, contributing to their overall effectiveness. In relation to cultural practices such as child sacrifice or widow burning, they engaged in a direct prophetic *critique* of the actions, along with the values, social structures, and ideas that supported the actions. The Bible is always the ultimate social critic, empowering Christians to become effective critics of their societies. On the other hand, in relation to certain issues, the Christians in their circles in India *created* new cultural practices that arise from our central Christian convictions. Examples of new cultural creations would be the way they sent girls to school and the manner in which they buried their dead. Additionally, there were ways in which the missionaries made significant *contributions* to the cultures of India, which had a legitimacy and value outside of Christian circles, regardless of the faith or unbelief of the people who benefited from these contributions. Good contributions to the cultures were the grammars and dictionaries of multiple languages, some of which were greatly needed, while they also published newspapers, which served the common good. And at the same time, Christian preachers almost always *correlate* the healing good news of Christ with the deepest human needs, as those needs are experienced within the terminology of a particular culture. Even when not clearly articulated, this answering correlation of the gospel with human need is usually central to mission motivation. These multiple methods of relating the Bible to the cultures of India formed an organic part of the tremendous holism seen in the truly classical mission work of Carey and his team.

So read about William Cary and be challenged to this type of holistic mission. Imitate his courage, love, creativity, and endurance. But also consider the patterns in his mind and in his knowledge of God's truth that led to this holistic mission work. This is a crucial need of the twenty-first century.

The Calvinism of William Carey

And Its Effect on His Mission Work

By Dr. Terry G. Carter

Dr. Terry G. Carter is Associate Dean and teaches Christian History and Ministry at Ouachita Baptist University in Arkadelphia. He received his undergraduate degree from Howard Payne University and his MDiv and Ph.D. from Southwestern Theological Seminary in Ft. Worth, Texas. He has written or co-written The Journal and Selected Letters of William Carey (Smyth & Helwys, 2000), Preaching God's Word (Zondervan, 2005), Telling God's Story (Broadman & Holman, 2006) as well as numerous articles dealing with Christian history, preaching, and ministry for journals and magazines.

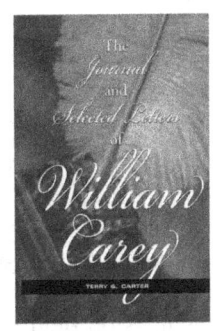

This paper was read at the Evangelical Theological Society meeting in 2001 and updated for this volume in 2010.

Introduction

William Carey was born August 17, 1761 into a confused and divided English religious setting. He spent his early years as part of the Church of England but as a young man switched to the Calvinistic Particular Baptists. True spiritual life for Carey was initiated during his teen years by the persistent witness of a fellow cobbler's apprentice named John Warr. Following his conversion William Carey fully involved himself in spiritual things including a deep concern for his family. He was from the beginning a believer who took evangelism seriously.[5] John Warr continued to influence his friend and on February 10, 1779, convinced Carey to attend a dissenter's worship meeting. He heard Thomas Chater, a Baptist, preach on the cost of discipleship. Chater became an influential friend to Carey, recommending him to a church and taking him to his first Baptist associational meeting in 1782 in Olney.[6] Carey became an active part of Particular Baptist life.

---

[5] Timothy George, *Faithful Witness: The Life and Mission of William Carey* (Birmingham: New Hope, 1991), 8.
[6] Ibid., 10-11.

His influence would be spectacular. Soon Carey was asking if it was the duty of modern Christians to publish the gospel in every place of spiritual darkness across the world. He wrote An Inquiry into the Obligations of Christians, to use Means for the Conversion of the Heathens (1792) which challenged Baptists to consider the requirement to pray for God's kingdom to come and his will to be done as a mandate not only to verbally witness but also to "use every lawful method to spread the knowledge of his name."[7] In the Fall of 1792 Carey's dream expressed in the Inquiry to establish a society for the express purpose of supporting foreign missions became reality. That event started a mission movement across the evangelical world.

But how did Carey accomplish this? Carey was a Calvinist, but many other Baptist Calvinists in England at the time would not have dared such a thing. Carey's Calvinism was different from that common to most Particular Baptists in England in the 1700's. The focus of this study will be to examine the Calvinism of William Carey, the Father of the Modern Mission Movement, and determine how that theological stance affected his work on the mission field in India. First, a look at the theological setting of Carey's day will be necessary in order to understand the predominant hyper-Calvinism among Particular Baptists so we might fathom the uniqueness of Carey and his friends. Second, a study of the sources of William Carey's brand of Calvinism seems appropriate as no one develops a personal theology in a vacuum. Finally, the study will evaluate how the Calvinistic beliefs of Carey were reflected in his mission work. This section will rely heavily on the Journal and letters of Carey to observe the theological tenets of the missionary as they surfaced in his everyday life.

The Calvinism of the 1700's in England

During the 1700's an extreme form of Calvinism (hyper-Calvinism) developed. John Gill, a Baptist, represented this form of Calvinism and became its key spokesman among the Particular Baptists. Gill published often and always maintained the sovereignty of God as the cornerstone of his theological system. He viewed God as sovereign in everything including the activity of salvation. As a result, Gill refused to offer Christ to unregenerate sinners. Gill's system viewed election as "free and sovereign; God was not obliged to choose any; and as it is, he chooses whom he will...and the

---

[7] Ibid., E.3.

difference in choosing one and not another is purely owing to his will."⁸ God's election of others to damnation was just as intentional and binding.⁹ John Mockett Cramp, a Particular Baptist in Kent and later Canada, described this system a century later.

> "They were supra-lapsarians, holding that God's election was irrespective of the fall of man. They taught eternal justification. Undue prominence was given their discourses to the teachings of scripture teaching the divine purposes...They were satisfied with stating men's danger, and assuring them that they were on the high road to perdition. But they did not call upon them to repent and believe the gospel. They did not entreat them to be reconciled unto God. They did not warn and teach every man in all wisdom. And the churches did not, could not, under their instruction, engage in efforts for the conversion of souls. They were so afraid of intruding on God's work that they neglected to do what he had commanded them. They seem to have supposed that preservation was all they should aim at; they had not heart enough to ask for extension. No wonder that the cause declined."¹⁰

This hyper-Calvinism devastated Particular Baptist life. In 1715 one historian listed 220 churches in England but 35 years later (1750) that number fell to only 146. Most of those churches were half the size. For instance, the Norwich church reported 52 members in 1723, but only 27 in 1750.¹¹ This climate was hardly ideal for a mission movement. It was a harsh Calvinism that emphasized the sovereignty of God and the hopelessness of the non-elect as "foreordained to condemnation, whose names were left out of the book of life." It hardly made sense to Gill and other hyper-Calvinists to offer gospel invitations for them to become Christians.¹² In fact the task of the church was merely to receive the elect and nurture them in the faith.¹³ A new kind of Calvinism would have to evolve for a Carey to fulfill his dream.

---

8 H. Leon McBeth, *The Baptist Heritage: Four Centuries of Baptist Witness* (Nashville: Broadman Press, 1987), 176-77.
9 Ibid.
10 W. T. Whitley, *Calvinism and Evangelism in England, esp. in Baptist Circles* (London: The Kingsgate Press, 1930), 27-28.
11 McBeth, 172-73.
12 Ibid., 177.
13 Willaim H. Brackney, *The Baptists* (Westport, CT: Praeger Publishers, 1994), 40.

The Sources of Carey's Evangelical Calvinism

William Carey entered the Particular Baptist church at a time when he was trying to make sense of his new faith and develop his personal theology. At the same time the hyper-Calvinism of Gill was under heavy attack. Intelligent and able pastor/theologians were beginning to question the conclusions of the supra-lapsarians. Surely there was another way to approach the biblical view of sovereignty and election. Particular Baptists like Alevery Jackson, pastor at Barnoldswick in Yorkshire, reorganized his church on the basis of a new evangelical Calvinism which held that all men have the duty to believe in Christ.[14] Abraham Booth published the Reign of Grace. He argued that God takes no delight in the misery of people and has a higher end in mind.

> "Complete provision is made for the certain salvation of every sinner, however unworthy, who feels his want, and applies to Christ. The gospel is not preached to sinners, nor are they encouraged to believe in Jesus under the formal notion of their being elected. No: these tidings of heavenly mercy are addressed to sinners, considered ready to perish."[15]

These men were part of the new culture of evangelical Calvinism that was beginning to grow in influence. In this culture Carey worked out his own theology. Two men seem to have had the most influence on Carey's development theologically – Robert Hall and Andrew Fuller. Both were good friends and wrote treatises on the subject of Calvinism that became to Carey and others pivotal writings. A consideration of each seems warranted.

Robert Hall of Arnsby

Robert Hall of Arnsby served as one of William Carey's theological guides. As Carey attempted to work out his Calvinism he was loaned a copy of Hall's Help to Zion's Travellers. This work helped Carey to put together the pieces of his own theology. In addition, Carey became friends with Hall who became his mentor in the ministry.[16] But it was Hall's writing that allowed Carey to solidify his theological system. Carey claimed that prior to Hall he had merely the Bible as his source. In Help to Zion's Travellers Carey found

---

[14] Whitley, 29.
[15] Ibid., 35.
[16] S. Pearce Carey, *William Carey* (London: The Wakeman Trust, 1923), 58.

> "...all that arranged and illustrated which (he) had been so long picking up by scraps. I do not remember ever to have read any book with such raptures as I did that. If it was poison, as some then said, it was so sweet to me that I drank it greedily to the bottom of the cup; and I rejoice to say, that those doctrines are the choice of my heart today."[17]

Hall outlined his view of Calvinism in the book. In addition, Hall purposed to remove stumbling blocks which cause the traveller to Zion to stumble – things that would be "injurious to the people of God."[18] Hall was a Calvinist but he reinterpreted it. He saw the hyper-Calvinism of the day to be one of those injurious obstacles.

A summary of Hall's Help to Zion's Travellers gives us insight into what put it all together for Carey. Robert Hall believed in the main tenets of Calvinism. He held to the total depravity of mankind including its devastation of the image of God in man.

> "As all mankind have lost the image of God in which they were created, and become base and abominable in his sight, being filthy and guilty before him, they must have continued in a condition eternally disgustful to God, and in a state tremendously terrible to themselves..."[19]

Despite this dreadful condition, Hall allowed that man is free to choose, but unfortunately, sinful man will not choose God or good. To choose correctly man must have the operation of the Holy Spirit to change his bias and disposition to evil. When a man is regenerated by the Spirit he will be changed to will and work to do God's good pleasure. He is still a free man but now chooses good.[20]

As most Calvinists, Hall based his theology on the sovereignty of God. Even God's love for mankind is sovereign. Hall considered this a significant point. The love of God, which elects humans is sovereign and not natural love. The objects of the love do not deserve it, but despite that they are voluntarily favoured because of this love. God's necessary hatred of sin is not contrary to sovereign love or the gracious intentions to do good to his people.[21]

---

[17] Eustace Carey, ed., *Memoir of William Carey, D.D.* (London: Jackson and Walford, 1836), 16-17.

[18] Robert Hall, *Help to Zion's Travellers* (Boston: Lincoln, Edmand's and Co., 1833), 25-27.

[19] Ibid., 50.

[20] Ibid., 231-42.

[21] Ibid., 50-51.

God's sovereignty also included the common Calvinistic doctrine of election. Election implied three things: the freedom of the elector, election always for a purpose, and the person chosen is considered passive and at the will of the elector. Hall distinguished between election to an office like David or Samuel and the election of grace. Election of grace consists of choosing persons in Jesus Christ for salvation through sanctification of the Spirit.[22]

Some rejected election saying it was negative because the non-elect would be automatically reprobate. Hall insisted election was not the opposite of reprobation and did not hurt the non-believer.

> "Election or choice, indeed implies a negative, or that some are not chosen; which the Scripture calls the rest; this is readily allowed, but reprobation as mentioned in Scripture is never opposed to election. To the doctrine of election it does not seem related, but stands in a quite different situation in the system of scriptural divinity."[23]

Reprobation is not the opposite of election because election is an act of divine sovereignty arising from the will of God without any desert in the people elected. Reprobation represents a deficiency or defect in a person. Election flows from the good will of God to his people while reprobation is not from God's will but from a natural contrariety between the purity of God and the pollution of the reprobate. God does not accept them for this reason. In essence they are not saved due to their own sinful disposition, which opposes God's will and purity.[24]

Concerning a union with Christ Hall spoke of a threefold nature – visible, vital, and virtual. Visible referred to a credible profession of Christ and apparent obedience such as church membership or attendance. However, visible believers were not automatically considered Christians. The vital union consisted of a divine connection to Christ, which takes place at regeneration. This category was truly in the Christian realm. They possessed the sensation of sin and guilt, the work of the Spirit in them causing them to strive against sin, and the preservation, which comes from Christ.[25]

---

[22] Ibid., 61-63.
[23] Ibid., 68.
[24] Ibid., 69-75. "But as everyone who perishes suffers only according to the demerit of his own personal sins therefore to infer that the doctrine of election is detrimental to man, and unworthy of God, discovers either pitiable weakness, or powerful prejudice." Ibid., 75.
[25] Ibid., 78-84.

Hall posited an unusual view of adoption and regeneration as regards salvation. In his scheme adoption preceded regeneration. It is the preparation of the Spirit in the life of the unbeliever.

> "Adoption constitutes relation, but does not convey likeness of nature; but regeneration does both. Adoption is before, or antecedent to regeneration, for there is not propriety in supposing those are made sons by adoption who are so by birth...Adoption is the act of God's sovereign will, according to Eph. i. 5, 6."[26]

Adoption represented that initial work in the non-believer intended to draw them to God.

But the key question of the day was the "Modern Question" or "Whether it be the duty of all men to whom the gospel is published, to repent and believe in Christ?"[27] The answer to this question would open or keep doors closed to evangelism and missions for Particular Baptists. Hall had an answer and it was a resounding yes. He explained.

> "Their right to come to Christ does not in the least depend upon, or arise from, a prior knowledge or interest in special blessing, or feeling themselves the subjects of supernatural principles...If anyone should ask, Have I a right to apply to Jesus the Saviour, simply as a poor, undone, perishing sinner, in whom there appears no good thing? I answer, Yes; the gospel proclamation is, 'Whosoever will let him come.'"[28]

This became the justification of the evangelical Calvinists to issue invitations and conceive of missions. Perhaps Carey owes his own vision to this answer of Hall. Certainly for Carey the invitation, "Whosoever will let him come" became central.

Of course for Hall, this in no way negated the sovereignty of God in the process. God through the Holy Spirit still initiated and made the individual capable of belief and commitment.

> "But when omnipotent grace begets new principles in the soul, changes the Heart, and opens the understanding to behold things as they really are, then the world and all temporary good sinks in to nothing and vanity, when compared with Christ and the blessings of the gospel. Now the will which before freely chose sinful delights, as freely chooseth the one thing needful. Christ, in whom sinners saw no form or comeliness wherefore they should desire

---

[26] Ibid., 91.
[27] Whitley, 29.
[28] Hall, 129.

him, is now in their esteem the chief among ten thousand, and altogether lovely...Now they freely choose the paths of virtue and religion, as before they did those of vice and sensuality."[29]

Hall maintained God's sovereignty and allowed Christians to offer salvation to the unregenerate and the unbeliever to seek Christ. By Carey's own admission Hall's work impacted him greatly. A young pastor seeking direction discovered a teacher.

Andrew Fuller and "Fullerism"

If Robert Hall stood tall in Carey's theological education, perhaps one stood taller – Andrew Fuller. Carey and Fuller shared a deep respect and friendship that lasted until Fuller's death in 1815. Fuller fought the same theological struggle Robert Hall battled. He grew up in the hyper-Calvinistic tradition and discovered his own election by God. On a visit to London in 1775 Fuller came across a pamphlet by Dr. Abraham Taylor concerning the Modern Question. He remarked that "it revived his doubts on what was called the High Calvinistic system, or the system of Dr. Gill, Mr. Brine, and others as to the duty of sinners, and of ministers addressing them."[30] In addition, Fuller had the advantage of good friends such as Robert Hall, John Sutcliffe, and John Ryland, Jr. who were also struggling with this strict Calvinism.

Eventually Andrew Fuller put his beliefs into print in a book destined to become enormously influential among Particular Baptists and others. In his *The Gospel Worthy of all Acceptation* (1785) Fuller set out to present scriptural principles to combat false views of Calvinism. Much of this grew out of his own conversion experience, which he described purely as grace. "I saw plainly, that my salvation must be, from first to last, of free grace." Fuller believed the doctrine of grace had been abused and set out to reinterpret the Calvinism of the day.[31]

> "Like Robert Hall, Andrew Fuller stood clear on the "Modern Question." Unbelievers are to believe in Christ. In Part II of his work Fuller outlined his position.
> I. Unconverted sinners are commanded, exhorted, and invited to believe in Christ for Salvation...

---

[29] Ibid., 160.
[30] McBeth, 181.
[31] John W. Eddins, Jr., "Andrew Fuller's Theology of Grace" (Th.D. diss., Southern Baptist Theological Seminary, 1957), 5, 8.

> II. Every man is bound cordially to receive and approve whatever God reveals...
> III. Though the gospel, strictly speaking, is not a law, but a message of pure grace; yet it virtually requires obedience, and such an obedience as included saving faith...
> IV. The want of faith in Christ is ascribed in the Scriptures to men's depravity, and is itself represented as a heinous sin...
> V. God has threatened and inflicted the most awful punishments on sinners for their not believing on the Lord Jesus Christ...
> VI. Other spiritual exercises, which sustain an inseparable connexion with faith in Christ, are represented as the duty of men in general..."[32]

Fuller believed people are depraved but have a duty to come to Christ and believe in him. God's sovereignty plays a major role in this belief. The Holy Spirit must do a work of regeneration in the sinner which included a restoring of the soul to purity. The Holy Spirit produces a change in the form of a holy disposition of the heart that is miraculously wrought in depraved man by the irresistible grace of God through the Holy Spirit. The Holy Spirit in essence opened the eyes of the lost man to see. "A blind man must have his eyes open before he can see..."[33]

> "Like Hall, Fuller allowed sinners to come to God while maintaining the sovereignty of God. The genius of Andrew Fuller was that while he examined the doctrines of Grace in the light of the scriptures, he was able to maintain the dialectical Tension between God's sovereignty and the other aspects of grace as the scriptures indicated it to be. Therefore, since he found more revealed emphasis on the God of sovereign grace in man's salvation, that the sovereign God of election and reprobation, he was able to correct the abuses of hyper-Calvinism."[34]

In addition Fuller held on to the doctrine of election. John Eddins in his dissertation on Fuller's doctrine of grace summarized his issues with hyper-Calvinism.

> "1. The doctrine of election and all other discriminating doctrines of grace remain in effect.
> 2. The invitation, which is extended to sinners to participate in God's spiritual blessings, is not designed to convince them they are entitled to the

---

[32] *The Complete Works of the Rev. Andrew Fuller: With a Memoir of his Life, by Andrew Gunton Fuller,* ed. Joseph Belcher, vol. II (Philadelphia: American Baptist Publication Society, 1848), 343-60.
[33] Eddins, 192.
[34] Ibid., 250.

blessings as long as they remain in unbelief.

3. The issue is whether the law "does not require every man cordially to embrace whatever God reveals."

4. There is no dispute about whether men should believe more than the gospel presents, but whether what is in the gospel should be believed with all the heart.

5. The question is not whether sinners are able to believe but if they are under some kind of inability.

6. It is not a matter of whether faith is the ground of acceptance of God but whether it is not required as the appointed means of salvation.

Finally the question is not whether unconverted sinners should be the subject of exhortation but whether they ought to be exhorted to perform spiritual duties."[35]

Apparently Carey accepted Fuller's explanations of Calvinism. He based His vision of missions on it. Fuller's favourite verse became the marching orders of Carey. "Go...preach the gospel to every creature: he that believeth and is baptized shall be saved; but he that believeth not shall be damned. Mark 16: 15-16"[36]

Jonathan Edwards and Freedom of the Will

Another key figure in the development of evangelical Calvinism in England was Jonathan Edwards. Timothy George states that "in many respects the writings of Jonathan Edwards were the single most important influence on Fuller, Carey, and the English Baptists who launched the missionary movement."[37] Eustace Carey described Edwards' influence in the *Memoirs*.

"Before Carey left England, he was deeply imbued with North American theology. President Edwards, its great master, was his admired author. The strong and absorbing view in which he exhibited some leading principles in the system of revealed truth, seemed so clearly to explode the errors of arminianism on the one hand, and of pseudo-calvinism on the other, and to throw such a flood of irresistible light on the mediatorial dispensation, as perfectly captivated, and almost entranced."[38]

Carey first read Edwards when a copy of "An humble attempt to promote explicit agreement and visible union of God's people in extraordinary

---

[35] Ibid., 43-45
[36] Ibid., 48.
[37] George, 49.
[38] Carey, 131.

prayer for the revival of religion and the advancement of Christ's kingdom on earth" was introduced to him by John Sutcliffe. This pamphlet moved the Northamptonshire Association to set apart an hour for prayer one Monday a month to pray that God would spread the gospel to the most distant parts of the globe.[39] Carey also read Edwards sermons for inspiration and information. He remarked "what a spirit of genuine piety flows thro that great man's works."[40]

Perhaps the most important work of Edwards for the English Baptists was *Freedom of the Will*. In the mid-1770's John Ryland Jr. read *Freedom of the Will* and was heavily influenced by its doctrinal teaching. He recommended the work to Fuller and Hall. The work became the basis for Fuller's *Gospel Worthy of All Acceptation*. Edward's distinction between moral and natural ability in man offered Fuller the key to reinterpret Calvinism. Natural ability is man's rational faculty and power to choose. Moral ability is the disposition to use natural ability to choose correctly. The lack of good moral ability causes man to choose poorly.[41] In addition, Edwards grounded human choice in motives, which direct the will. Man is capable of volition and choice – free to do what he pleases. However, his will is dominated by motives.[42] Edward's agreed that man is totally depraved and corrupt because his heart is under the power of sin, but God interposes on him sovereign grace which allows him to do good in God's sight.[43]

Considering the company he kept, William Carey was undoubtedly a Calvinist but not the strict variety of a John Gill. Carey inherited and embraced an evangelical Calvinism, which accepted the five points of Calvinism but with an evangelical flare that allowed bold and intentional invitations to sinners to accept the gospel truth believing that they are capable of responding. Election and the necessity of the Holy Spirit's work in the sinner was still in effect but a new Calvinism capable of spawning a missionary movement now existed among Particular Baptists in England.

---

[39] John Brown Myers, *William Carey the Shoemaker who Became "The Father and Founder of Modern Missions"* (London: S. W. Partridge & Co., 1887), 22.
[40] Ibid., 18, 22.
[41] E. F. Clipsham, "Andrew Fuller and Fullerism: A Study in Evangelical Calvinism" The Baptist Quarterly 20, no. 3 (July 1963): 110-11.
[42] Sang Hyun Lee and Allen C. Guelzo, editors, *Edwards in our Time* (Grand Rapids: William B. Eerdmans Publishing Company, 1999), 90-91.
[43] Paul Ramsey, ed., *Works of Jonathan Edwards*, vol. 1, *Freedom of the Will* (New Haven: Yale University Press, 1957), 432.

The Calvinism of William Carey the Missionary

Evaluating William Carey's Calvinism is not an easy task. Carey never wrote anything which resembled a systematic or for that matter purely theological treatise. He wrote volumes but always in the form of letters, apologies for missions, or reports from the mission field. Therefore, determining his Calvinistic beliefs becomes a task of gleaning and sometimes reading between the lines. This approach involves risk. When writing letters or journaling many people are not particularly careful with expressions or detailed meaning. Sometimes in conversational letters the writers use the rhetoric of their day or even clichés to communicate a message. Perhaps Carey was guilty of that. However, from extensive work in the letters and Journal of Carey I tend to believe he was more careful than most with his words. With that in mind we will plow through the Journal and letters of Carey to discover what Calvinism lurks there.

The Sovereignty of God

Like most Calvinists, Carey focused on the sovereignty of God above all other doctrines. In fact, God's ultimate control probably supported all Carey believed and he often mentioned the providence of God or God's action in the affairs of men including life, death, and spiritual issues. Carey preached a sermon on God's sovereignty, which he outlined for Fuller in a letter dated March 25, 1812.

> "To me the consideration of the divine sovereignty and wisdom has been very supporting and, indeed, I have usually been supported under afflictions by feeling that I and mine are in the hands of an infinitely wise God. I endeavoured to impress this our afflictions last Lord's Day, from Psalms XLVIE. 10 "Be still and know that I am God." I principally dealt upon two ideas, viz. 1. God has a sovereign right to dispose of us as he pleases, 2. We ought to acquiesce in all that God does with us or to us. To enable us to do which I recommended, realizing meditations upon the perfections of God, – upon his providence, and upon his promises including the prophesies of the extension of the kingdom."[44]

Carey believed in a God in full control of all that is. This became his explanation and perhaps pat answer for everything he, his family, or associates encountered in life.

---

[44] Carter, (Carey to Fuller, March 25, 1812), 257-58.

God's Sovereignty in the Ministry

Carey depended on the sovereign God completely in his ministry in India. Early on he experienced many frustrations and connected them to God's providence. In a Journal entry dated April 19, 1794 the missionary expressed his trust.

> "Well I have God, and his word is sure; yet my hope, fixed in that Sure Word will rise superior to all obstructions, and triumph over all trials; God's cause will triumph, and I shall come out of all trials as God purified by fire – Was most humbled today by reading Brainerd – O what depravity betwixt me and him; he always constant, I unconstant as the wind."[45]

For Carey God was the guarantee for the work. He opened the doors, supplied all the needs, removed the obstacles, and issued the results. When faced with a grave difficulty (Mr. Thomas, Carey's partner in missions had squandered the mission money leaving none for ministry and missionary support.) Carey relied on God's sovereign ability to take care of the situation.

> "I rejoice however that he is all sufficient and can supply all my wants, spiritual, and temporal, my Heart bleeds for him (Thomas), for my family, for the society whose steadfastness must be shaken by this report, and for the success of the mission, which must receive a sad blow from this; But why is my Soul disquieted within me, Things may turn out better than I expect, everything is known by God, and God cares for the mission – O for contentment, delight in God, and much of his fear before my Eyes…"[46]

In writing to Jabez, his missionary son, Carey encouraged him with the ability of God to deal with all difficult issues. He explained to his son that as a missionary he had been placed by God in the situation and should expect difficulties and discouragements "but the work you are engaged in is the work of God. He is the one who opened the way and removed previous difficulties." Carey assured his son that God would eventually crown his preserving efforts with his blessing.[47] In similar statements to Ryland Carey described the providence of God as a powerful force. "The openings of providence or rather loud calls of providence, are now very numerous and

---

[45] Ibid., 26.
[46] Ibid., (Journal entry, Jan. 23, 1794), 11.
[47] Ibid., (Carey to Jabez, Sept. 13, 1819), 70.

are continually increasing...the Lord has done great things for us, and far surpassed our expectations."[48]

Carey understood the regular receipt of supplies for the needs of the mission as a direct result of the providence of God. Carey insisted that God was directly involved in the monetary receipts of the mission.

> "The Cause of our Redeemer gradually gains ground, and the accounts from various posts are highly gratifying, especially from Benares, Dinadjpur, and Arrakan. The Lord has wonderfully appeared also in pecuniary things. Last Year The Benevolent Institution fell off so much in its Funds that it was Ten thousand Rupees in Debt. I made an application to Government for assistance, and they agreed to allow 200 Rupees a month for it. And within the last month a Man died at Dilbee, who was utterly unknown to us all; nor do I know that he was a Professor of Religion. His name was Dunn. He left 60,000 Rupees to his Wife during her life, and after her death 30,000 of it is to go to the Calcutta Free School, 10,000 to the Benevolent Institution, 10,000 to the Serampore Mission, 5,000 to the female Asylum, and 5,000 to the Parental Academies Institution. Thus we are witness to the kindness of God in finding means to support his own cause..."[49]

God's Sovereignty in Life and Death

Carey saw the hand of God in everything and that truth became his answer to issues of health, life, and death. He corresponded with his sisters frequently and often consoled them concerning issues of health. In sharing with them both as brother and it seems pastor, he most often connected their struggles with God's providential working. Carey tried to teach his sisters a bit of theology as he attempted to comfort them in their physical trials.

> "We are the worst possible judges of what things are really good things, for we generally suppose ease, prosperity, friends, and external enjoyments of health and plenty to be good things, whereas they may be either good or evil according to circumstances. God's judgment of what things are good, therefore, frequently differs from ours, for he often bestows those external, apparently good things on his Enemies, and visits his saints with poverty, disappointment, afflictions, contempt, and many other things supposed by us to be evil. He, however, well knows these external evils to be necessary to the

---

[48] Ibid., (Carey to Ryland, Nov. 17, 1813), 187.
[49] Ibid., (Carey to Sisters, Oct. 25, 1827), 214-15.

substantial good of his servants; and were not this the case they would not be exercised under them..."⁵⁰

God's sovereignty went beyond health and physical well-being. God was involved directly in death. On the mission field Carey and his companions encountered death regularly. Carey personally suffered the death of two wives, two children and several missionaries. These deaths did not occur accidentally – God was in the midst of them. One of Carey's most common phrases concerning death was "I am dumb with silence because the Lord has done it."

On one occasion Carey's son, Felix, lost his wife and two children in a storm at sea. Carey's response to this horrible tragedy was acknowledgement of God's work.

> "A little time ago I wrote to you by the way of Java particularly informing you of the distressing providence, which had befallen Felix. On the eleventh or twelfth of August as he with his family were going to Ava on a brig purchased for him at Calcutta, a squall came on and overset the vessel. Felix's wife and two children, a female servant and four men were drowned. Felix and the rest of the people swam to shore...I mourn for Felix in silence, and still tremble to think what may be the next stroke. I am dumb with silence because God has done it."⁵¹

Perhaps related to this discussion of God's providence in sickness, death and afflictions on people, Carey speaks often of God's discipline. Although this might not be distinctively Calvinistic, it seems to correspond to the involvement of God in all things. In a letter to Jabez, Carey mentioned a principle that would guide God's discipline on people. "I think Divine Providence generally returns improper conduct upon the heads of those who are guilty of it..."⁵² Carey suspected God was disciplining his son, Felix, for misconduct in his personal life and mission work.

> "We are every day expecting Felix. I long to see him but fear he has much declined in divine things. He is coming in some official situation, for which I am sorry. Had Felix continued firm to his object and laboured for the spread

---

⁵⁰ Ibid., (Carey to Sisters, Oct. 1818), 270. See also (Carey to Carapeit, July 2, 1819), 125.
⁵¹ Ibid., (Carey to Jabez, Nov. 25, 1814), 288. See also; (Carey to Fuller, Jan. 14, 1808), 287; (Carey to Ryland, June 14, 1821), 288; (Carey to Burls, Oct. 5, 1821), 289-90; (Carey to Jabez, Nov. 12, 1822), 290; (Carey to Sisters, Feb. 21, 1831), 104.
⁵² Ibid., (Carey to Jabez, May 15, 1812), 126-27.

of the Gospel I could have met every distressing providence with confidence that all would work for good, but I am now at every step full of apprehension and anxiety respecting what may be the next stroke of divine providence for the Lord is a jealous God and no one can be indifferent to his interests with safety."[53]

The Depravity of Man

Carey held the line with other Calvinists in arguing for the depravity of mankind. He saw this as a key area of missions and an obstacle to be dealt with. In a letter to Fuller in 1797 Carey suggested that there were only two real obstacles to missions on earth. One was the lack of the Bible. The other was the "depravity of the human heart."[54] Carey described this condition as a "miserable state of unconverted men, as spiritually poor, as bound by a sinful disposition, and by pernicious Customs, and false expectations of Happiness, from false Idolatrous Worship..."[55] He wanted to make everyone aware of this condition to show the need for salvation.

> "I have some time past contriving a plan of a Work, which I intend to write in Bengali. The design is to prove the Gospel is a most necessary blessing to them; on account of the TOTAL DEPRAVITY OF THEIR HEARTS, THE ENTIRE CORRUPTION OF THEIR CUSTOMS, and the INSUFFICIENCY and CONTRADICTION of the Books by them accounted SACRED."[56]

Carey argued that the mind of man was capricious, fallen and "justly exposed to the curves of that Law that is holy, & just, & good." Carey continued with his description of depraved man. "But the bias of our minds is opposite to that which it ought to be, and which in the nature of things cannot satisfy us, it proves that they who have no better portion will meet eternal disappointments."[57]

However, depravity for Carey was not hopeless. The depraved person can sue for mercy and gain it. God has made a way and the intelligent person will seek God's way and obtain salvation. In a letter to his Father before ever reaching the mission field Carey's evangelical Calvinistic view of man's situation becomes clear.

---

[53] Ibid., (Carey to Jabez, Feb. 1, 1815), 269.
[54] Ibid., (Carey to Fuller, March 23, 1797), 64.
[55] Ibid., (Journal entry, May, 9, 1795), 58.
[56] Ibid., (Carey to Ryland, August 31), 157.
[57] Ibid., (Carey to Father, April 26, 1788), 248.

"How should we live! By nature Children of Wrath and under Condemnation. How earnestly should we sue for mercy! Our Carnal minds at Enmity against God. How ought we to be sorry for our Sins! Repentance is necessary to salvation. Pardon, Justification, Adoption, Sanctification may all be obtained by asking for them, without them we are miserable; with then we shall be eternally Happy. How stupid are those who neglect them!"[58]

Depravity became for Carey a reason for the mission endeavour. Human depravity exemplified the need and urgency for all mission work.

The Doctrine of Election

No doubt Carey held to some form of this doctrine but his letters and Journal give little detail concerning it. One might suppose that his strong view of God's sovereignty would support speculation on the subject. In a conversation with an unbeliever, a Mr. Short, Carey explains to him the necessity of faith in Christ for salvation. Mr. Short called Carey "illiberal and uncharitable" because this excluded all unbelievers and committed the heathens to eternal misery. Carey argued that he "was no more uncharitable than the Bible, and that if that was the case, God would appear gloriously just."[59] It is unclear if the subject of election took centre stage in this conversation but some of the terminology seems familiar to the subject. Carey does not openly describe his view of election in his correspondence or Journal.

The writings of Carey indicate that he does not dwell on the idea of only some being elect. Instead his rhetoric concerning salvation is inclusive. Perhaps Carey did not want to muddle the mission goal with such theological discussions. His task clearly was to take the gospel to the lost just as he found them and let God sort it out.

It is common to read in Carey's work phrases of inclusiveness. In sharing a witnessing encounter with some natives Carey detailed in his Journal the conversation. "I then told them how God sent his son, to save Sinners, that he came to save them from Sin, and that he died in Sinner's stead, and that whosoever believed on him would obtain everlasting life, and would become Holy." Carey did qualify it a bit by saying "I told them that God was under no obligation to save any Man, and that it was of no use to make Offerings to God to obtain pardon of Sin...and that if God forgave them it must be from his own Will; but that he was willing to save for the sake of

---

[58] Ibid., (Carey to Father, March 3, 1787), 248.
[59] Ibid., (Journal entry, April 7, 1794), 22-23.

Jesus Christ."[60] Even toward the end of his life Carey retained the language of inclusiveness. Writing to his Sisters in 1831 he spoke of the availability of salvation.

> "And the acceptance of that sacrifice of atonement was testified by the resurrection of our Lord from the dead and by the commission to preach the Gospel to all nations with a promise, or rather a declaration, that whosoever believeth on the Son shall be saved, shall not come into condemnation, but is passed from death to life."[61]

If Carey was a strong believer in election he certainly did not dwell on it choosing to focus on the possibility of every individual being saved.

The Doctrine of Salvation

Carey's view of salvation was Calvinistic but not overstated. Salvation depended entirely on what Jesus did on the cross for sinners and how they responded to it. Everything turned on the atoning power of Jesus on the cross. Even in his latter years Carey proclaimed that his own salvation and the righting of all things wrong in the world depended on that atonement power.

> "I know in whom I have believed, and that He is able to keep what I have committed to him, against that day. The atoning sacrifice made by our Lord on the Cross is the ground of my hopes of acceptance, pardon, justification, sanctification, and endless Glory. It is from the same source that I expect the fulfillment of all the prophecies and promises respecting the universal establishment of the Redeemer's Kingdom in the World, including the total abolition of idolatry, Mohammedanism, Infidelity, Socinianism, and all the political establishments of Religion in the World; the abolition also of War, Slavery, and oppression in their ramifications. It is on this ground that I pray for, and expect the peace of Jerusalem; not merely the cessation of hostilities between Christians of different sects and connections, but the genuine love which the Gospel requires, and which the Gospel is so well calculated to produce."[62]

Salvation rests on the work of Christ on the cross and on that alone.

In a letter to Fuller Carey explained it further. All of us are sinners and absolutely helpless but there is good news. God in his rich mercy became

---

[60] Ibid., (Journal entry, Feb. 22, 1795), 53-54.
[61] Ibid., (Carey to Sisters, Oct. 25, 1831), 251-52.
[62] Ibid., (Carey to Sisters, Dec. 16, 1831), 260.

incarnate and lived more than thirty years on earth without sin. "He gave sight to the Blind, healed the Sick, the lame, and the Deaf and Dumb – and after all died in the stead of Sinners." We deserved the punishment of death for our sins but God endured it for us. We were unable to make any kind of atonement for our guilt but Jesus "completely made an end of Sin." He has now sent us to tell the world that the work is done and to call them to "faith in, dependence on the Lord Jesus Christ. Therefore, leave your vain customs, and false gods, and lay hold of eternal life through him."[63] For Carey salvation is based on the atoning work of Christ and requires faith in and dependence on Jesus.

Carey also believed that the depravity of mankind required the work of the sovereign God for salvation to be realized. In his Journal, Carey explained that God's Spirit must be involved in the sinner for belief to occur. "If once God would by his Spirit convince of sin, a Saviour would be a blessing indeed to them; but Human Nature is the very same all the world over; and all conviction fails except it is produced by the effectual working of the Holy Spirit."[64] Human depravity is such that there must be an external source of power for the conviction of sin. That source is God's Holy Spirit effectually working on the individual to bring him/her to that point. Carey believed this work of God's Spirit to express itself in evangelism. In a narrative about a witnessing event he explained the difficulty of getting the natives interested in the gospel at all. He was dejected because of their inattentiveness. Then the mood changed and Carey attributed it to the working of God. "I was however enabled to be faithful, and, at last God seemed a little more to fix their attention..." The natives then asked for weekly meetings to read the Bible and study it together.[65] God's involvement changed the situation.

Perseverance of the Saints

Occasionally William Carey sounded unsure of his own complete salvation. In a letter to his Father in 1807 he admitted this. "I am far from a confidence that I shall go to heaven when I die; but I wish to be found among them who will eternally love and serve God." Carey went on to say that he enjoyed the company of saints and even though he considered himself unworthy and the lowest spiritually, he *wished* to be in their presence forever.[66]

---

[63] Ibid., (Carey to Fuller, Nov. 1800), 149.
[64] Ibid., (Journal entry, Feb. 1, 1794), 15.
[65] Ibid., (Journal entry, Feb. 1, 1795), 51.
[66] Ibid., (Carey to Father, Feb. 18, 1807), 250-51.

As he aged Carey seemed to grow in his own confidence of perseverance in the faith. In 1816 at age 56 he softened the earlier uncertainty as he shared his feelings with Ryland in a letter. He noted that his dear friends Pierce, Sutcliffe, and Fuller had gone to their rest. He stated, "Whenever I die may I through divine Grace join them in the World of bliss."[67] As he neared his own death his confidence grew even more and the reasons for it were made clear. Writing to family members he expressed his confidence in persevering with God.

> "I am this day seventy years old, a monument of Divine mercy and goodness, though on a review of my life I find much, very much, for which I ought to be humbled in the dust. My direct and positive sins are innumerable, my negligence in the Lord's work has been great, I have not promoted his cause, nor sought his glory and honour as I ought. Notwithstanding all this, I am spared till now, and am still retained in his work, and I trust I am received into the divine favour through him...Indeed, I consider the time of my departure to be near; but the time I leave with God. I trust I am ready to die, through the grace of my Lord Jesus; and I look forward to the full enjoyment of the Society of Holy Men and Angels, and the full vision of God evermore."[68]

Carey's assurance was based on God and his grace. The next year, even closer to death, Carey tells Jabez of his confidence in final salvation. In spite of his sinful activities, he claimed assurance based on what he saw. "...But I see the atoning sacrifice of Christ to be full and complete, to have been accepted of God, and to be a ground...the bestowment of all spiritual blessings..." He based his future in scriptural truth. "Christ has said, 'He that cometh to me I will in no wise cast out.' My conscience bears witness that I do come to Christ and I feel the enjoyment arising from confidence in His gracious declarations."[69]

Summary of Carey's Calvinism

In the research I hoped to discover distinct Calvinistic doctrines clearly stated. But Carey was a missionary, not a theologian. He invested his life continuously in the practical application of God's truth. This is not to imply that Carey was at all anti-intellectual and uninterested in theology. His Calvinism was merely that on which he acted. He trusted implicitly in the

---

[67] Ibid., (Carey to Ryland, Dec. 30, 1816), 258.
[68] Ibid., (Carey to Jabez, Aug. 17, 1831), 260.
[69] Ibid., (Carey to Jabez, Sept. 3, 1832), 261.

sovereign nature of God in virtually every area of life and ministry. Other Calvinistic doctrines are not as easily interpreted in Carey's writings. He certainly held to the idea of depravity in humans but his view of this did not exclude the ability of the sinner to respond to God and therefore his responsibility to share the gospel. Carey defined salvation very much like a modern evangelical might but with little detail. He spoke of it mostly in context of his mission work with sinners. He never spoke explicitly of election. Carey believed in perseverance based on God's promises and grace and he was the example. He made Calvinistic proclamations when speaking on God's sovereignty but when dealing with salvation he often sounded like an Arminian. Of course, he, Fuller, and Hall had been accused of that before.

Conclusion

The type of Calvinism William Carey inherited from men like Hall and Fuller was an active and compassionate type. It was evangelical in every way. His theology never stopped him from evangelism and missions, but rather it catapulted him into these endeavors. When he thought about his beliefs he could do nothing but act on them.

> "Had some serious thoughts this morning upon the necessity of having the mind evangelically employed, I find it is not enough to have it set upon Duty, Sin, Death or eternity. These are important but as the Gospel is the way of a sinner's deliverance, so Evangelical truth, should and will, when it is well with him, mostly occupy his thoughts."[70]

In fact, Carey's system of theology caused him to question why anyone would hesitate to think evangelically when considering sinners and their need for salvation. In the beginning of his mission work, Carey wrote to his good friend, John Ryland, about his full commitment to the work of evangelizing the world. "The worth of souls, the pleasure of the work itself, and above all the increase of the redeemer's kingdom are with me motives sufficient, and more than sufficient to determine me to die in the work, that I have undertaken."[71] It baffled Carey that not everyone would feel this way. Writing to his Father in 1805 he expressed his concern. "On a review of what we do we often wonder how it is that persons who are

---

[70] Ibid., (Journal entry, June 3, 1794), 32.
[71] Ibid., (Carey to Ryland, Dec. 26, 1793), 69.

under such strong obligation should feel so little love to, and do so little for the Saviour who has done so much for us."[72]

Carey's theology is probably best reflected in his life. He believed in a powerful, involved, sovereign God who loved sinners and desired them to become his own children. God provided all things necessary for that to happen and sent out his servants to proclaim the good news and invite sinners to respond. This became William Carey's life and passion. The Calvinist Carey was the evangelical Carey.

Bibliography

Ahlstrom, Sydney E. *A Religious History of the American People.* New Haven: Yale University Press, 1972.

Brackney, William H. *The Baptists.* Westport, Connecticut: Praeger Publishers, 1994.

Carey, Eustace. *Memoir of William Carey, D.D.* London: Jackson and Walford, 1836.

Carey, S. Pearce. *William Carey.* London: The Wakeman Trust, 1923.

Carter, Terry G. *The Journal and Selected Letters of William Carey.* Macon: Smyth & Helwys Publishing Inc., 2000.

Clipsham, E. F. "Andrew Fuller and Fullerism: A Study in Evangelical Calvinism, Part I 'Development of a Doctrine'." *The Baptist Quarterly* 20, no. 3 (July 1963): 99-114.

Drewery, Mary. *William Carey: A Biography.* Grand Rapids: Zondervan Publishing House, 1978.

Eddins, John W. "Andrew Fuller's Theology of Grace." Th.D. diss., Southern Baptist Theological Seminary, 1957.

Fuller, Andrew Gunton. *The Complete Works of the Rev. Andrew Fuller.* Edited by Joseph Belcher. Vol. II. Philadelphia: American Baptist Publication Society, 1848.

---

[72] Ibid., (Carey to Father, July 11, 1805), 69.

George, Timothy. *Faithful Witness: The Life and Mission of William Carey.* Birmingham: New Hope, 1991.

Hall, Robert. *Help to Zion's Travellers.* Boston: Lincoln, Edmand's and Co., 1833.

Lee, Sang Hyun and Guelzo, Allen C., editors. *Edwards in Our Time.* Grand Rapids: William B. Eerdman's Publishing Co., 1999.

McBeth, H. Leon. *The Baptist Heritage: Four Centuries of Baptist Witness.* Nashville: Broadman Press, 1987.

Meyers, John Brown. *William Carey the Shoemaker.* London: S. W. Partridge & Co., 1887.

Ryland, John. *The Life and Death of the Rev. Andrew Fuller.* Charlestown: Samuel Etheridge, 1818.

Simonson, Harold P., ed. *Selected Writings of Jonathan Edwards.* Prospect Heights, Illinois: Waveland Press, Inc., 1970.

Smith, George. *William Carey: Shoemaker and Missionary.* London: J. M. Dent & Sons, 1909.

Tull, James E. *Shapers of Baptist Thought.* Valley Forge: Judson Press, 1972.

Whitley, W. T. *Calvinism and Evangelism in England, esp. in Baptist Circles.* London: The Kingsgate Press, 1930.

William Carey's Contribution to Indian Languages

By P. Sam Daniel, Ph.D.

Professor at the ACTS Academy of Higher Education, Bangalore, India

Reprinted with permission by the editor M. S. Thirumalai reprinted from the journal "Language in India", Volume 1:2 (April 2001), see http://www.languageinindia.com/april2001/carey.html

1. William Carey (1761-1834)

William Carey was born in England in 1761, arrived in India in 1793, and died in Serampore, near Kolkata (Calcutta) in 1834. Carey had very humble beginnings. He was only a shoemaker, rather a cobbler as he used to say, since he was only mending the shoes of others. But his love of people all over the world, born out of his love of Jesus Christ, and his passion to preach the gospel of Jesus to all the nations, led him to India. He had such passion for knowledge early in his life that he taught himself Latin and a few other subjects. Over the years this love of people and Jesus helped him to learn several Indian languages and enabled him to translate the Bible into many languages of north and east India. He was first introduced to the Indian languages through Bengali, which he learned while working as a manager of an indigo factory in a Bengali village. He also had the help of a musnshi to learn Bengali and Sanskrit. From the beginning the goal of Carey was to translate the Bible into Indian languages. So, as soon as he started learning the Bengali language and Sanskrit and had developed some confidence regarding the structures and words of these languages, he started the translation of the New Testament into Bengali. In the process Carey became an excellent grammarian and lexicologist of many Indo-Aryan languages, but it soon turned that his translation skills were far behind his knowledge of grammar and lexicon.

2. Protestant Missionary Assumptions Regarding Language Use

One of the important assumptions of the Protestant missionaries has been that "non-Christian peoples must be approached in their own language. For that reason the missionary must possess as good a knowledge as possible of the local forms of speech" (Neill 1985:191). It is also expected that "the missionary must be sedulous to acquaint himself with the mind and customs of the people among whom he dwells" (Neill 1985:192). A third assumption of the early missionaries to India was that "in a land where the vast majority of the inhabitants are illiterate, (the widespread diffusion of the Gospel among the peoples of India) can be achieved only by oral proclamation" (Neill 1885:192). These assumptions were questioned by the leading Catholic missionaries of the time. Abbe Dubois, for example, questioned the wisdom of translating the Bible (especially the Old Testament) and distributing the copies among the Hindus and Muslims, because, according to him, the translations were not only imperfect but often stopped the Hindus from wanting to know more about Jesus because they did not find anything therein that would make them to give up their religion in preference to Christianity. On the other hand, a strong theological position of the Protestant missionaries has been that the Bible "is in itself the great instrument for the conversion of non-Christians, and that therefore it must be made available to Indians, Christian and non-Christian alike, at the earliest possible date" (Neill 1985:195).

3. The Translation Strategy Adopted by Carey

Carey's strength lies in envisioning the need and to go after fulfilling that need. He recognized the fact that India is populated by different linguistic groups and that each of these groups needs to be given the translation of the Bible in their own tongue. He also realized that the Indian vernaculars were yet to be fully developed as vehicles of learning. The Protestant missionary assumptions demanded that the Bible be made available in the vernacular. Sanskrit was the preferred medium and target of learning in most parts of India in the traditional schooling system, and the modern Indian languages were struggling to find their own place. During the Mughal rule, Persian became the official language of the rulers, and Hindustani developed into a powerful medium of interaction, but the regional languages of north India had not received much official patronage for their development. There was the need for the Christian missionaries to take the gospel of Jesus Christ to the multitudes of people and this desire on their part coincided with the need and thirst for the development of the Indian vernaculars.

Carey's love for the Bengali vernacular, (he thought that Bengali is intrinsically superior to all other spoken Indian languages, Neill 1985:191), did not stop him from seeing the importance of Sanskrit, especially for the translation of the Bible into various Indian languages. Carey learned Sanskrit for many years, and translated parts of the *Ramayana* into English.

His plan was to first translate the Bible into Sanskrit and use this reliable version for translation into other Indian languages. In several ways this plan was to be lauded. Translations of the theological concepts, names of the characters in the Bible and places, controlling the nuances of the terms used through a dependence on the Sanskrit terms were some of the advantages of this approach. It may not be out of place to point out that such similar techniques would be followed by the various Kranth Academies in India after independence. He hoped that, after the translation of the New Testament into Sanskrit in 1808, "the work could now be extended to all the languages of which Sanskrit is the parent" (Neill 1985:195).

That this strategy is now increasingly questioned by the translators of the Bible does not minimize the practicality of the design. A translator does not work as an island. He seeks information and terms from various sources. Often the translation in an adjacent language helps him to arrive at the right word to represent faithfully the theological intent of the word under translation. While it is true that most of Carey's translation is now passed over, no body could deny that his was a valiant attempt and that because of his attempt to coherently present long texts in prose closer to the spoken language, modern Indo-Aryan languages of India were blessed.

4. Carey's Contribution to Bengali

My focus in this paper is only the contributions made by Carey to Indian languages. (I do not deal with Carey's involvement in the controversy regarding the introduction of English as the medium of instruction in schools around the country. Carey took the position that is appealing to most of us today. At that time, however, the terminology to refer to that concept was *European education.* Carey argued that in the schools European education should be the substance, but the vernacular, the medium or the vehicle for imparting that education.)

Through the publication of *Bengali Colloquies*, written with the help of Bengali scholars, Carey showed the power of the colloquial Bengali as an effective medium of communication. It is Carey, more than any other European scholar-missionary, who really showed to the natives of India that prose could be an effective medium. As Thirumalai (2001, in his forthcoming article in *Language in India*) shows, long ago, in south India, Ziegenbalg, the first ever Protestant missionary to India, took upon himself the onerous task of translating the Bible into Tamil. He chose the medium of prose for his translation much against the traditional practice of saying profound things through the medium of poetry. It was the necessity to preach the good news of Jesus Christ to all, not just the educated or upper classes, that made him to choose the medium of prose for the translation of the Bible. It was the very same necessity that forced these translators to base their translation on the colloquial language rather than on the formal style of the language. Moreover, the Bible itself was written mostly in prose. But these missionary-translators went one step further: even where the Bible had in its original poems or poetic language, these translators chose to translate these pieces in ordinary colloquial language, mostly in order to achieve communicative efficiency.

Just this act of choosing prose as the preferred form for expressing messages in long texts has enabled the modern Indian vernaculars to cross the traditional boundaries and break into a new world and establish their identity. It has enabled every literate Indian to compose his thoughts in writing without the cultivated exquisitiveness of poetry and express himself in much easier way.

Carey was instrumental in translating the Bible into Marathi, Hindi, Oriya, Panjabi, Assamese, and Gujarati. While others did help, Carey was also totally involved in all these translations! Carey learned Telugu and Kannada to bring out the translations of the Bible in these languages. Later on work on Pashto and Khasi were undertaken. On a rough estimate we may say that Carey either worked or influenced heavily the translation of the Bible into as many as thirty five languages. And in all these languages and dialects (several translations were made in to the "dialects" of Hindi). Carey was breaking new grounds and laying the path for the development of these languages as vehicles of education. It is no wonder than that Rabindranath Tagore, himself a master of Bengali, wrote: "I must acknowledge that whatever has been done towards the revival of the Bengali language and its improvement must be attributed to Dr. Carey and his colleagues. Carey was the pioneer of the revived interest in the vernaculars" (Carey 1923).

Das Gupta writes: "A living language can never be regulated by artificial rules borrowed from a dead language, however closely connected they might be with each other and Carey in giving full scope to colloquial and temporal variations, shows himself fully alive to this fact ... yet one can never wholly dispense with Sanskrit grammarian framing a grammar for its vernacular offshoot. A truly scientific grammar of Bengali must avoid these extremes and Carey who had a wonderful knowledge of the vernacular as it was spoken and written as well as of the classical Sanskrit, succeeded to a great extent in steering through the middle path" (Das Gupta 1993).

5. To Conclude

William Carey came to India because he loved the people and wanted to share the gospel of Jesus Christ. He was not personally successful in converting the Hindus and Muslims to the Christian faith in large numbers. In fact his score on this count is next to nothing! That did not deter him from finding other avenues of service to His Lord and to the people he came to serve. Through the translation of the Bible and through his various other publications he enriched modern Indian languages, encouraged prose as the preferred medium of expression for education, introduced a strategy of translation based on Sanskrit, and established procedures of translation such as team work. But he was not satisfied by all these linguistic efforts, which came so naturally to him.

Carey pioneered selfless work against certain social practices such as infanticide and sati (suttee). Along with his colleagues, John Marshman and Ward, Carey had been unremitting in his endeavor to draw the attention of the government to the practice of sati. Support received in the person of Raja Ram Mohan Roy brightened the prospects for the abolition of sati. Carey with the help of the learned pundits connected with the Governor-General's College in Calcutta, collected from the Hindu sacred books the passages upon which this custom was believed to have been raised. These investigations showed him that sati was a rite simply encouraged as a virtue and not enjoined as a duty (Marshman 1873:99). The vernacular newspapers pioneered by the Serampore missionaries were used to enlighten the minds of the Indians. At length, their continuous fight against this practice paved the way for the abolition of suttee (Caree 1923:334).

"Carey was preparing to preach, a courier from the Governor-General arrived with an urgent dispatch, an order in council which Carey was requested immediately to translate into Bengali. It was nothing less than the famous edict abolishing suttee throughout British dominions in India. Springing to his feel and throwing off his black coat he cried, **"No church for today!"** Without the loss of a moment he sent an urgent request to one of his colleagues to take service, summoned his pundit and then settled down to his momentous task. For twenty-five years he had been urging the necessity of this law and there should be no further loss of time and life – if he could prevent it. "If I delay an hour to translate and publish this many a widows' life may be sacrificed," he said. "By evening the task was finished" (Walker 1951:252-253).

Carey was not just a great linguist, but a great lover of people and God.

References

Carey, Pearce. 1923. *William Carey*. New York: George H. Doran Company.

Das Gupta, R. K. William Carey and Bengali Grammar. In J. T. K. Daniel and R. E. Hedlund, (eds.) 1993. *Carey's Obligation and Indian Renaissance*.

Walker, R. Deaville. 1951. *William Carey, Missionary, Pioneer and Statesman*. Chicago: Moody Press.

William Carey: Using God's Means to Convert the People of India

George Ella

Dr. George M. Ella was born in England in February 1939, and as a teenager moved to Sweden to continue his training as a Forestry Apprentice. After his conversion he returned to England to study theology. Whilst at the London Bible College, he attended the worship services of the well-known Dr. Martyn Lloyd-Jones. Upon graduation at London and Hull Universities, he worked as a school teacher and evangelist among the Lapps. For the past 32 years Dr. Ella has lived in Germany, near the Dutch border. Now retired, his career included work as a Senior Civil Servant, university examiner and writer of curricula for librarian assistants and apprentice retailers for the state's commercial colleges. This work included editing and grading textbooks. After adding various external degrees and post-graduate qualifications in theology/literature, business studies, education, history, psychology and library science at Uppsala, Duisburg and Essen universities, he gained a doctorate in English Literature at Duisburg University. He has written a number of books prior to this volume, including works on William Cowper, James Hervey, John Gill, Andrew Fuller, William Huntington and Augustus Toplady. Dr. Ella was nominated for the John Pollock Award by Prof. Timothy George in 2001. A major work on the English Reformation Exiles under Mary I will appear shortly. Dr. Ella has authored numerous biographical essays and doctrinal studies which have appeared in magazines such as the Banner of Truth, the Banner of Sovereign Grace Truth, the English Churchman, the Baptist Quarterly, Focus, New Focus, the Bible League Quarterly, and the Evangelical Times.

Primary publication

Part One: How Carey Became a Missionary

The search for an historical Carey

Ever since 1966 when my Professor of Missions at Uppsala, Bengt Sundkler,[73] presented his students with facsimiles of Carey's *An Enquiry into the Obligation of Christians to use Means for the Conversion of the Heathen* and told us vivid tales of Carey's forty years in India, this great missionary has been one of my fondest mentors. Prof. Sundkler said he had learnt from Carey to drop all fastidious controversy and put the Church of the Lord Jesus Christ before formal denominationalism. Following Carey's good Christian example, Sundkler became a missionary to Africa and was

---

[73] Author of *Missionens Värld*, 1963 etc.

given the post at Uppsala after his retirement. However, though a Sundkler, a Culross, a Myers, a Pearce Carey, a Jones, a Bullen, a Walker, a George and a Webber have written on Carey, such as myself feel that the full true life of this godly man has still to be portrayed. Indeed, as each author describes Carey from his particular view-point only, I often think that it would take a well-researched joint-work by many authors both male and female to do full justice to Carey's memory. Even then, the danger would be that such authors would compromise on essential features of Carey's life so as to avoid controversy. Carey himself protested that while his work was not yet done and it was far too soon to evaluate the overall impact of his mission, churches, denominations, missionary societies, political parties and philanthropic societies were already inventing 'lives' of him which were pure fiction. Sadly, most modern evaluations have been built on these 'lives'.

Carey's home background

William Carey was born in the village of Paulerspury, Northamptonshire on August 17, 1761, the first of Edmund and Elizabeth Carey's five children. Edmund was a weaver who also kept a small school and acted as parish clerk. William learned to read, write, study the Scriptures and enjoy Bunyan's *Pilgrim's Progress* at an early age. He was brought up as an Anglican and was to find Christ in that church under the preaching of Thomas Scott, friend of Cowper and Newton. William's uncle Peter, a much travelled man who had retired from the army to devote himself to gardening, engendered a great interest in foreign countries and horticulture in his nephew through his adventurous tales. As a child, William was allergic to strong sunshine which made his parents feel that he could never visit those sunny countries made so enticing by his uncle. He was therefore apprenticed to a shoemaker at the age of 14, a trade which occupied him for the next 28 years.

At a time when Carey confessed that neither Heaven nor hell interested him, John Warr, a fellow-apprentice and Dissenter, lent him Christian books which prepared him for Scott's preaching. Thus Carey grew to respect both the Church of England and Dissent. This caused him some difficulty when faced with the narrow-mindedness of many of his friends and supporters in later years. However, in the days and environment of his youth, the 'dipped and sprinkled' to use Cowper's language, 'lived in peace'. This was because John Bunyan had been active in Northamptonshire, Buckinghamshire and Bedfordshire and the Dissenting Meeting Houses there met according to the rules 'Water-baptism no bar to communion' and thus practiced 'open communion' with their brethren. However, in 1764 six churches joined to form the Particular Baptist Association and by 1779 when Carey began to fellowship with those of John Bunyan's persuasion in Hackleton and Olney, the immersion issue had become prominent and several churches chose to become members of the Association and practice immersion, though they remained divided rather than open on the communion issue. However, John Sutcliff (1752-1840), one of the first immersionist pastors at Olney, still fellowshipped with Anglican Evangelicals. This was mainly because a long succession of sound ministers including Moses Brown, John Newton, Thomas Scott, C. Stephenson and Henry Gauntlett ensured that Olney had an Evangelical pastor for the major part of the 18th century. It was a common Olney sight to see Sutcliff taking an evening stroll arm in arm with the Olney vicar and his curate. Olney church records tell of his preaching the Gospel in the plot of land between John Newton's Vicarage and William Cowper's Orchard Side, assisted of course by Newton. Anglican Cowper writes of the great spiritual times he had with the new Baptist denomination of which he says, "It was a comfortable sight to see thirteen gospel ministers together. Most of them either preach'd or pray'd and all that did so approved themselves sound in the Word and doctrine, whence a good presumption arises in favour of the rest. I should be glad if the partition wall between Christians of different denominations would every where fall down flat as it has done at Olney." Needless to say, all these ministers were invited to dine with Newton at the Vicarage.

Life at Olney and district

Carey wrote later in his *Memoir* that it was at this time that he was enabled "to depend on a crucified Saviour for pardon and salvation; and to seek a system of doctrine in the Word of God." After conversion, Carey was gradually convinced of the need for believer's baptism by immersion and was subsequently baptised by John Ryland Jr. (1743-1825) in the River Nene on October 5 1783. His wife of two years, Dorothy (Dolly) Packet, an Anglican believer, did not join him in this act. Now, through the persuasion of John Sutcliffe (1752-1840), Carey became a member of the Particular Baptist Church at Olney, established by John Bunyan in 1672. He immediately applied to be set apart as a preacher but the church did not feel he had the ability and turned him down after a trial sermon in the summer of 1785. By this time Carey was preaching outside of the denomination and had recently accepted a call to Moulton Baptist church on a salary of £12 per year without the blessing and official sanction of his own pastor and church. His wages were inadequate to support Carey and his growing family so the trustees of the Particular Baptist Fund kindly allowed Carey a grant of £5 a year.[74] Nevertheless, Carey was still compelled to work in his trade and serve as a schoolmaster to top up his earnings. In order to teach his pupils geography and foreign mission work, he made a globe for them out of scraps of leather. Carey's Moulton work was crowned with a number of conversions so a year after his initial disappointment, Carey was accepted with 'unanimous satisfaction' for the ministry by the Olney congregation, who, nevertheless placed him on a further year's probation. Then, on 1 August, 1787, Carey was at last ordained 'to preach wherever God in his providence might call him'.

The Careys' first child, Anne, died in her second year but their remaining children, Felix, William and Peter developed as healthy, sturdy boys. In October, 1787, Dolly underwent baptism by immersion, performed by her husband. Carey's interests, however, were far wider than Moulton and he began to collect information concerning the spiritual state of the whole world, writing his comments on a large home-made map he had hung up in his workshop. World-wide geography became his passion, fuelled by a copy of Cook's *Voyages* and works on the growth of the British Empire. Reports of societies for the Indian mission formed by Phillip Jacob Spener (1635-1705) and August Hermann Franke (1663-1727) in Denmark and Germany thrilled Carey as also tales of Count Zinzendorf (1700-1760) and the Moravian missionaries to the Caribbean, North American, Greenland and Abyssinia. Carey had also followed the stories of John Elliot's and David Brainerd's mission to Native Americans. He made himself familiar with the appeals of Independent Philip Doddridge in the seventeen-forties for the evangelisation of the world and the calls for prayer concerning such a world-wide ministry amongst the Presbyterians of America and Scotland. He studied carefully the Anglican missions to the New World. He was in agony at the thought that the Baptists were lagging behind. Gradually, Carey was putting together statistics for his famous *Enquiry*. Realising that a missionary, especially one who was prepared to give his flock the Bible in their own language, must be fluent in the Biblical languages, Carey diligently studied Greek and Hebrew,[75] assisted by Sutcliffe. Carey then added Dutch and French to the classical languages. One day, a Christian merchant named Gotch who provided the army with Carey-made boots asked his business partner how much he was now making a week. Nine to ten

---

[74] A normal pastor's wage at the time was £60-100 per annum. Samuel Pearce, for instance, received £100 p. a. from his church.

[75] He had begun learning Latin years earlier.

shillings was the reply. Gotch then told Carey to stop making boots and he would provide him with ten shillings a week to allow him more time for language study. Another friend, on hearing that Carey was withholding publication of his *Enquiry* because of funds, gave him £10 towards costs. Finding that 28 year-old Carey could still hardly keep his family on under £20 a year, the Moulton church in 1789 encouraged him to accept a call to Harvey Lane, Leicester, a larger church. The salary turned out to be only slightly more than at Moulton so Carey had to return to boot-making. He soon heard that his successor at Moulton had demanded and was receiving a higher salary.

Ripening for the mission field

All was not well at Harvey Lane. The church had gone through three pastors in as many years and such were the fierce controversies that many left when Carey was appointed, though he had been assured that total harmony prevailed concerning his call. An Antinomian spirit in the church led to gross immoralities being condoned by the prominent members. Then, the Careys' daughter Lucy died before reaching her second birthday. On the brighter side, Carey made friends with a group of Christian scientists and philanthropists in the city who helped greatly in Carey's wider education, especially by giving him the use of their libraries. The immorality at Harvey Lane increased, so Carey disbanded his church and drew up a new membership list. Many old members repented and joined the new church which now grew by leaps and bounds. Only then did Carey feel himself ready for his official inauguration which was conducted by Ryland, Samuel Pearce (1766-1799), Andrew Fuller (1754-1815), and Sutcliffe. Pearce had a strong desire to go to India as a missionary and shared his plans with Carey. During the next Association meeting at Clipstone, Carey, supported by Pearce, put forward his proposals for a foreign mission society. Sadly, his proposals were rejected.

Carey published his *Enquiry* in 1792 which moved many to think again concerning world evangelism. When 24 association churches gathered at Friar Lane Nottingham in May, 1792, Carey was the chosen preacher. His sermon moved, blessed and thrilled all as Carey urged his hearers to expect great things and attempt great things of God. Nevertheless, the majority of ministers hesitated to support Carey's plea to train and send out missionaries to the foreign field. Carey was in agony and in the final minutes of the meeting begged Fuller to make a proposal to save the cause. Fuller immediately moved "that a plan be prepared against the next ministers' meeting at Kettering, for forming a Baptist Society for propagating the gospel among the heathen." The day was far spent and the delegates were eager to get home, so the motion was quickly passed and Carey began to breath normally again.

The formation of the Mission Society

The Kettering meeting on 2 October was something of an anti-climax. Only twelve ministers, a student and a deacon gathered at Mrs Wallis' home, fondly called *The Gospel Inn* to discuss the society. Only one minister, Pearce, attended from outside the local association. Most of those present were more against the project than for it, chiefly because they felt the richer churches, who were not present, should take the initiative. Then Carey stirred the 'nobodies from nowhere', as Pearce Carey calls them, into more Christian thinking by relating current stories of the Moravian missionaries and their success amongst Native Americans and Africans. Carey emphasised that the Moravian harvesters, some of whom were British, were poor men who had learnt that they could do great things through the riches of God's mercy. Finally, a resolution was moved, signed by all present to form the *Particular Baptist Society for the Propagation of the Gospel amongst the Heathen* with Carey, Sutcliff, Ryland, Fuller and Reynold Hogg (Thrapsten) as executives. Thus the Baptist mission to foreign heathens did not start as a church or denominational movement but as a parachurch organisation with a limited executive. Once Carey began founding local churches, the absentee executive insisted on controlling them. Spurgeon protested strongly that the Baptist Mission Society allowed anyone to join it, provided they paid a membership fee of 10s 6d. But still this was a start and Carey was able to use his own discernment and prevent too much society influence, though he had to drop his open communion plans through Fuller's dogmatism.

As yet, however, the society had no idea of whom they would send out or where they should go. They made a collection but few had any money with them so promises, instead of cash, were put into a snuff-box passed round. These amounted to £13. 2s 6d. However, once the society was formed, more substantial gifts came in from Christians around the country from all denominations. The people of Yorkshire were especially generous and the poor blind curate of Bradford willingly parted with a guinea on hearing that the gospel was to be spread abroad. His Vicar followed likewise. Many Baptist ministers complained, arguing that the home churches were destitute and ought to be supported with such monies.

The call to India

Meanwhile, a letter arrived from a missionary to Bengal named John Thomas who was on a fund-raising tour and had intended to visit the Kettering meeting but had forgotten the time. He suggested that he and the new society should join hands and funds and they could provide him with a companion missionary. Fuller was commissioned to go to London and check out on Thomas. The letter-writer was a man of great abilities who had studied medicine, had been something of a rake, was permanently in debt and could not be trusted with anyone's money, not even his own. To escape poverty, he had signed on as a ship's surgeon on an India-bound vessel, leaving his wife and family to look after themselves. He became converted in India and felt a great compassion for the multitudes of Indians. He was probably the first Englishman to take the gospel to the Bengalis and master their language. He could live like an Indian amongst the Indians and translated several gospels into Bengali. Amongst his many converts were English noblemen and high cast Brahmins. Thomas, in spite of his new life in Christ, always lived far beyond his financial means. Fuller approached Thomas most naively. He was so thrilled to meet a real live missionary as if this gave Thomas a super-human status. Without a word about his many failings, Fuller recommended Thomas as God's opening door for the society and urged them to back him. Thomas, a brilliant speaker, visited the society on January 9 1793, saw and conquered and left the society dazzled and amazed. The matter of his great debts was concealed from those who were asked to support him. On being told that a missionary could easily provide for himself on the mission field, Carey volunteered to be the companion Thomas needed. He had already stated in his *Enquiry*, that if missionaries were provided with "clothing, a few knives, powder and shot fishing tackle and the articles of husbandry" necessary "to cultivate a little spot of ground just for their support", they could maintain themselves. He merely expected from the society that they should give missionaries sent out this initial support. Carey had lived simply at home and did not wish to live any finer abroad. Though Sutcliffe and Ryland were absent, the remaining executives entered formally into partnership with Thomas. Fuller, rather apprehensively, wrote to the executives not present to tell them, "It is a great undertaking, but surely it is right."

On returning to Leicester, Carey informed Dolly of his decision and intention to depart for India immediately. She refused point blank to allow Carey to go. He was in too poor health and she was eight months' pregnant. Carey's church also rebelled. Carey's father said his son had 'the folly of one mad'. All came round to accepting Carey's call. Dolly eventually promised to follow her husband in three or four years when their unborn child would be old and strong enough for the exhausting journey. So Carey would not be entirely estranged from his family, Dolly told him to let eight-year-old Felix accompany him.

The valedictory fiasco

Thomas and Carey planned to sail in March 1793 but after their valedictory meetings and tearful departures from their loved ones, they met with farce-like obstacles. A government clamp-down on private adventurers going to India made the missionary candidates fear they would be refused permission to sail. Influential Baptists advised Carey to pin no hope on gaining a permit. Carey then turned to 'good old father Newton' with his political associates. Could he risk travelling illegally to India? Newton sat on the fence and like Gamaliel in Paul's case, said, "Conclude that your Lord has nothing there for you to accomplish. If he have, no power on earth can prevent you." This ambiguous statement moved Carey to risk travelling illegally. The party thus boarded a ship in London and sailed to Portsmouth where a protection convoy was to join them. Then Carey discovered that Thomas was on the run from his creditors who were taking legal steps to stop the party leaving the country. Thomas was escorted to London to sort matters out and Carey had to face extra expenses caused by the delay. Meanwhile, he preached in the Baptist and Independent churches along the coastline. On 6 May, Carey heard that Dolly had delivered a healthy child and wrote that he could not be with her as his sense of duty overpowered all other considerations. He could not help telling her that Mrs Thomas, though delicate, was making the journey, feeling it was only right to accompany her husband.

Thomas returned on 23 May in time to see the ship sail off with Carey, Felix and Mrs Thomas standing forlorn on the jetty. The captain had been ordered to leave the missionaries behind because of Thomas' debts. Carey now returned home to Dolly and promised he would never leave her again. Now the positive side of Thomas' character rose to the surface. Within a week, he had raised money, reconciled himself with his creditors, discovered a ship which would carry them legally to India and organised the transport of their baggage. On hearing that Carey had given up his missionary plans, Thomas dashed to Carey's home and pleaded with his whole family so successfully that Dolly relented and agreed to accompany Carey to India with her children and her sister. Now Fuller drew back. The society could not pay for the large party and Thomas' 'debts and embranglements' frightened him. Then Yorkshire and London friends came to the rescue and Thomas quickly found new sponsors and through his enormous energies and powers of persuasion, soon had the party in Dover, ready to board – but the ship was nowhere to be seen. Nigh panic gripped the friends again but after a further delay of two weeks, the belated Danish ship glided into the dock. On 15 June she set sail for India with the missionaries and their families safely on board. The time of anxiety and chaos was to end for a while.

Part Two: Early Pioneer Work

Initial difficulties

When Britain pulled out of Egypt, a national newspaper featured a large cartoon of Egyptian ex-patriots sailing back home, throwing their wigs, spectacles and false teeth overboard. They were done with these marks of 'British civilisation' and wanted to return to the simple life. Likewise, as soon as the *Kron Princessa Maria's* sails were set, Carey took off his ill-fitting gentleman's wig and sent it sailing into the brine. From now on he would live the simple life of the Indian peasants in order to win them for Christ. Only death would sever him from his new home-country.

Carey used the five months' journey[76] wisely to learn Bengali and as he studied, he used his knowledge of Hebrew to assist Thomas in his Bengali translation of Genesis. His first opportunity to witness on board was not to an Indian, however, but to a French Deist who constantly ridiculed Carey's faith. The ship's Captain and owner, a naturalised Dane of British stock, known to all as 'Captain Christmas',[77] proved a good and faithful friend. He used his Danish connections to make sure that Carey and his family would be warmly received by the Scandinavians in Bengal. The Captain allowed Carey and Thomas to preach freely on board but the interest shown was limited to half a dozen people. As these included a Fleming, a Norwegian, a Dane, a German and a Frenchman, Carey saw this as the start of his world-wide mission. Storms made it impossible to enter any of the ports on the way so Carey could not send letters to the Society with his encouragements that they should press on to find missionaries for Africa, South America and China. He suffered terribly from seasickness but prepared letters asking the Society for Bible literature and gardening handbooks.

---

[76] 13. June – 11. November, 1793.
[77] Otherwise J. Smith.

On arrival in India, the missionary party were faced with immediate arrest or deportation by the British authorities as they again found themselves labelled 'unwanted'. Captain Christmas had them smuggled out of the ship on a small fishing boat which took them to Calcutta where they were welcomed by hospitable Indians. Carey was amazed how willing the Indians were to hear Thomas preach the gospel and he soon believed that missionaries would be welcomed wherever they went in India. Carey and Thomas quickly found a faithful fellow-missionary in Kiernander, an eighty-year-old Swede, who had dedicated his life to evangelising the Eurasians. Kiernander advised the English newcomers to set up their first station at Bandel. Thomas was dismayed to find that in his absence his former converts and especially Ram Ram Basu, who became Carey's teacher, had been scorned and ostracised by the British Christians and some of them had reverted to their former ways.

Carey makes himself independent of Society aid

Unwisely, the Society had entrusted Thomas with the £150 which were to cover the first year's expenses. Instead of catering for the basic needs of the missionaries, Thomas used the funds to hire a large city house with servants to 'keep up appearances' so that he might practice as a doctor and thus hopefully pay off his debts. This action forced the mission itself into debt and though Carey turned to English Christians in Calcutta for help, they refused to oblige him with a loan because of Thomas' reputation. Carey then sought secular employment as a botanist but was turned down. This was all too much for Mrs Carey who became more and more depressive. Felix became so ill with dysentery that he was at death's door. The Indians, through Ram Ram Basu's influence, came to the missionaries' rescue and found a rent-free plot of gardening land in the Sundarbans near Debbatta. An English official, Charles Short, then offered the Careys accommodation nearby. Carey now strove to keep his family by growing vegetables, hunting and fishing but Thomas remained a financial problem. The better climate and more abundant supply of food soon rid the family of dysentery and Carey actually confessed that he had never been happier. Seeing how successful Carey was in producing food, several hundred Bengalis who had fled from the area because of bandits and tigers, returned and became Carey's neighbours and his parish. Now Carey was living as a native with native Bengali's around him but instead of staying in the situation he had dreamed of for years, he allowed Thomas to influence him in leaving his demi-paradise. Thomas had been offered a post as an indigo producer with a substantial salary and had managed to persuade the Commercial Resident, a Christian man, to find such a post for Carey, too.

After an initial period of instruction in Malda and Goamalti, Carey and Thomas were placed in charge of the indigo factories in Mahipal and Mudnabati, Thomas taking the larger and Carey the smaller production centres. Carey's salary, however, was very substantial and as he would also earn commission on all sales, he believed that his initial aim to be financially independent of any home support was now fulfilled. He therefore wrote to Fuller and Ryland:

"I now inform the Society that I can subsist without any further monetary assistance from them. I sincerely thank them for the exertions they have made, and hope that what was intended to supply my wants may be appropriated to some other mission. At the same time it will be my glory and joy to stand in the same near relation to the Society, as if I needed supplies from them, and to maintain with them the same correspondence."

Nevertheless, after declaring his financial independence from the Society who had not provided the Careys with anything near the support they needed anyway, Carey asked them to kindly order a long list of tools and provide for an annual shipment of trees, shrubs and vegetable seeds which he would pay for out of his own pocket. Carey also told the Society that he was hoping to offer employment to those Indians who lost their cast through coming under the gospel. So now, Carey was an independent missionary, able like Paul, to earn his own keep and still minister to others.

The Society drifts away from Carey's *Enquiry* concept

The Society was not entirely to blame for their hitherto scanty support for their missionaries. Carey had not been able to send post home throughout the entire five months journey and he was anxious to assure his English friends that all was well in India before writing. Indeed, his first letters from India arrived well over a year after his departure and much of the original enthusiasm for Carey's *Enquiry* concept had subsided, replaced by the fear that the party had had a hostile reception in India and perhaps all were now dead. The Society was also rapidly developing ideas of their own importance and responsibility as a missionary administration body which did not agree with Carey's. The uncertainty as to the success of the mission had seriously affected Fuller's nerves and, after two weeks of partial facial paralysis, he found himself "incapable of reading and writing with intense application." Highly-strung Fuller melodramatised this as a sign that he was being martyred for the gospel and his country's sake, writing in 1793, "Upon the whole, however, I feel satisfied. It was in the service of God. If a man lose his limbs or his health by intemperance, it is to his dishonour; but not so if he lose them in serving his country. Paul was desirous of dying for the Lord; so let me!" Fuller was forgetting that it was the Careys who were facing starvation, deprivation and dysentery in India during that time and not he. Actually when the news came that Carey was safe and a mission was truly established in India and the realisation that the Society must make the next move, it left them in something of a panic. They were still much in doubt as to just what the Society was supposed to do and how they should go about doing anything. Home support was still at a minimum in comparison to the varied and ambitious plans some of the committee members had. Furthermore, the Society had formed the idea that the missionaries' work was an extension of their own church work in England, with 'native' churches being placed completely under the care and administration of the Society as their home base. More and more we find Fuller exercising a political, patriotic attitude to the East Indian Mission, as he called it, feeling that the more the Indians turned to God, the better support they would be for the East Indian Company and British rule in India. Thus, Fuller viewed his serving the mission as the best way to serve the expansionist interests of his country. How different were such views to those of his contemporaries William Cowper and John Newton as expressed in their letters and Cowper's great poems *Expostulation, Charity, Hope and The Task*! They saw liberty of body, heart and soul as one of the key outcomes of true missionary work and campaigned for a free India, divested of Colonial shackles. Carey makes it clear in his *Enquiry* that the gospel cannot be divorced from religious and political liberty and his *Introduction* begins with the admonition 'to use every lawful method to spread the knowledge of His name.' Carey's vision for the Baptist Missionary Society, alias the East Indian Mission, was quite different from the policies which the home team had now developed

The Society's plan was impractical from the start as the idea of 'home churches', was subsiding amongst the Fullerite branch of the Particular Baptists and being quickly replaced by an interest in 'Associationalism'. However, the associations were obviously far less enthusiastic about the Indian mission than Sutcliffe, Pearce, Ryland and Fuller. So, too, these associations gradually allied with the Arminian Baptists leading to the founding of the Baptist Union. This, in turn, brought on the great Downgrade of doctrine against which brave Spurgeon fought in vain. Fuller stated in 1814 that there were eleven association churches in Nottinghamshire and Leicester in all with an average of seventy members each, of which only fifty per church were 'truly Christian people'. In these churches there were still a diminishing number of influential Particular Baptists who viewed the Society's para-church organisation and methods of financing by canvassing outside of the churches, associations and denomination with well-grounded suspicion.

The Society's New Divinity

So, too, the Committee members began to tempt the churches away from the view of evanglising sinners practiced during the Reformation and Great Awakening. This met with stalwart opposition and fellowship in many churches was destroyed. Though Fullerite propagandists tell us perpetually that under Fuller new churches were established this was not through evangelical outreach or spiritual revival but through secession. The truth is; those who withstood Fuller's new teaching grew three times greater than the Fullerite churches.[78] Several counted thousands as their hearers. Thus, a good percentage of those who initially supported Carey's mission in any way were being rapidly alienated by Fuller's lax view of Biblical evangelism based on natural law and duty faith. William Button, a founder supporter of the Society felt compelled to write his *Remarks on the Gospel Worthy of all Acceptation* against Fuller and Ryland. The Anglican Evangelicals and High Calvinists, whom Fuller acknowledged were more successful evangelistically than he, believed that Fuller had abandoned the doctrines of grace, and thus looked on the organisers of the Society with suspicion. Dr Ryland's church shrunk in proportion to the amount of Fullerite influence on his preaching. Ryland's father had had a swift-growing church and his theology was represented by Gill's commentaries which were placed in the church building for all to read. This proved an embarrassment to Ryland Junior who had the commentaries removed when he took over from his father and began to force out those of Gillite faith and learning. Fuller's own church were soon complaining that they had an 'absentee vicar' as they were greatly neglected by their pastor who was often away on Sundays canvassing for money. The fact is that Fuller's Northamptonshire Association whose theology he had pioneered, was the first Particular Baptist Association to go Liberal, declare in 1889 that, "A few indeed, still cling to the theory of verbal inspiration, in spite of its being manifestly contrary to the facts."

After 1780, the leading Baptist and Anglican magazines began to point out the danger of Fuller's new philosophy, even calling it a gangrene in the churches. Furthermore, a number of those who stood closer to Fuller, such as Benjamin Beddome, believed that churches who were neglecting their

---

[78] From seven in 1830 to 33 in 1870.

own local work were hardly in a position to send out missionaries to do better abroad. Joseph Kinghorn, a supporter of and collector for the Baptist Mission, was shocked to find Fuller wished to silence any theological enquiry which might oppose his views. When Dr Ryland passed some of his own writings on to Fuller without his permission, Kinghorn was greatly upset when he heard that Fuller rejected them as the work of a man 'without modesty and sobriety' who was an 'infidel objector', merely because Kinghorn preferred freedom of conscientious enquiry to a suppression of it.

The Society's reaction to Carey's letter

Though Abraham Booth pronounced Fuller lost because of his new theology and especially his rejection of the doctrine of imputation, he nevertheless supported Fuller's idea of a Society's sovereignty over the mission field which it opened for the gospel. Thus, when Carey's letter speaking of his financial independence from the Society reached England on 5 August, 1794, Abraham Booth declared that the Society's short life had terminated abruptly because Carey had not asked them permission for his move into secular employment. Those who hoped that the Society still had a future, advised the Committee to drop Carey and India and send 'real' missionaries out to Africa. Oddly, enough, Thomas, who had initiated Carey's move, did not receive half the criticism.

Not wishing to take drastic measures, the Society wrote to Carey, naively and patronisingly, begging him not to go back into the world. Carey lovingly replied that he had made it quite clear to the Society that a true missionary should identify himself fully with the country to which he was called and make himself as independent as possible so as not to be a burden on anyone. It was Carey's honest opinion that struggling and begging for money from all and sundry could not possibly enhance the Lord's work but when a missionary was able to pay his own way, he was then freer to preach the gospel. Carey estimated that the indigo production would only demand his entire energies for three months in the year and even this would not be without his Christian witness. He could then spend the remaining nine months evangelising and teaching. Furthermore, Carey told the committee that thanks to his income he could pay for the printing of the Scriptures in Bengali and Hindustani. He knew they would have to admit that the Society was in no position to pay for the printing themselves. Pierce Carey, William's great-grandson, argues rightly that if the missionaries had waited for the needed support from the Society, they would have starved long before it came. Indeed, the few goods and monies which were being sent to India were taking, because of mismanagement, blunders and unreliable curriers, three years to reach India.

Though communications between India and Britain improved greatly, the positive and negative influences of the Society on the Indian Mission quite cancelled each other out. Though at times, help came form Britain when it was urgently needed, at other times, the home Society severely curbed and hindered Carey's missionary endeavours. The Society never understood Carey's theology of missions and this is still a much neglected area of study. Thomas Shirrmacher, in a rare attempt to outline Carey's missions theology,[79] shows how almost all modern Missionary Societies look back on Carey as their founder but contrary-wise hold to a theology of missions which was never his. Carey obviously stayed initially within the Baptist Society because of close friendship with its committee members, but he emphasised more and more the indigenous nature of his work in contrast to the younger generation of missionaries who had colonial and political ideas abhorrent to Carey and unbecoming to the gospel.

Carey continues doing it his way

Meanwhile, Carey was spending every weekend, several evenings a week and the entire rain period when the factories were closed, walking some 20 miles a day through pathless jungles to preach to the two hundred villages in the Company's district. By 1795 he could preach at length and the people heard him gladly but they did not, as yet, change their ways. Their centuries-old traditions made them willing to hear but slow to understand and slower still to change. So, too, becoming a Christian for the Bengalis meant being declared casteless and facing acute social restrictions. Full members in the small mission church thus remained white but there were a number of conversions amongst the Danes and British. Sadly, Ram Ram Basu began to live an adulterous life and was convicted of embezzlement. On the positive side, John Fountain arrived from England to join the missionaries. Sadly, Fuller took a strong dislike to Fountain for political reasons, feeling he was disloyal to the British Establishment and his letters to Fountain were full of condemnation with no encouragement in them in support of Fountain's strong desire to win souls for Christ. Fuller's interference became so extreme that Carey had to write to him telling him that his aggressive attitude to Fountain was 'near to killing' the new recruit. Unlike Fuller, Fountain left his politics out of his missionary strategy and Pierce Carey tells us that "Carey was very drawn to him (Fountain), as a

---

[79] *Aufbruch zur modernen Weltmission: William Carey's Missiontheologie.*

true yokefellow." A Portuguese of independent means from Macao, Ignatius Fernandez, was converted through Thomas' ministry and joined the missionaries in their work. He assisted in financing many projects and equipped the missionaries with new books and household necessities. At his death, wealthy Fernandez left most of his land and property to Carey's Mission.

Carey could now preach Bengali more fluently than Thomas and had begun to preach in Hindustani and was also studying Sanskrit believing the language provided a key to Indian cultures, traditions and thought processes. Early in 1797, he revised Thomas' translation of Matthew, Mark, Luke 1-10 and James and put the finishing touches to the rest of the New Testament, but the printing posed a major problem. Buying type in England was out of the question but his employer, Mr George Udny, generously provided the £46 for a press with vernacular type which was on sale in Calcutta. In 1799, Carey witnessed the horrible scene of a *Sati* or widow-burning which made him more determined than ever to win the Indians for the gospel. This prompted him to pray more urgently for fellow-workers. In May of that year Carey received a letter, posted over seven months previously, from William Ward who had once met him briefly at Goat Yard Church, Southwark. Ward wrote that he wished to live and die with Carey and was setting out forthwith for India *'with the others'*! Who the others were, he did not say. As the British government had banned missionaries from entering British India, Ward and *the others,* i.e. the Marshmans, the Grants and Brunsdon, had boarded an American ship bound for Danish Serampore.

Part Three: Harvesting at Serampore

The end of the Mudnabati mission

Just when all seemed well for the mission, a whole series of grave discouragements occurred. Of the five years Carey worked at Mudnabati only two had produced good harvests and the rest had been ruined by alternate droughts, storms and twenty-foot deep floods. Added to this, severe epidemics took their toll of the native workers. Thomas gave up the work in despair and so Mr Udny decided to close both Thomas' and Carey's plantations. Carey's plans for a mission financially independent of the Baptist Society's support were now in danger and he thought again of borrowing money to add to his own savings so that he could buy an indigo plantation himself. Udny, however, a man who had supported Carey's missionary work with great enthusiasm, was removed from his post and a fierce opponent of Carey's missionary plans replaced him. The East India Company, on the whole, now believed that the work of the missionaries was counter-productive to their aims in India. Though Lord Mornington strove to stop Sunday sports and trading, he nevertheless thought it in the interest of the Company to outlaw all 'private' printing presses. This was virtually a ban on publishing the Scriptures in British India. These disappointments appeared too great for Thomas and he began to estrange himself more and more from the work of the Mission. Then Carey heard that the new missionaries had landed at Serampore and placed themselves under the protection of the Danish flag but the British authorities had immediately demanded that Ward, Grant, Brunsdon and Marshman should be sent back to England. They feared that the Danes would fit them out with passports so they could preach unhindered throughout Bengal. Carey heard, too, that the women missionaries had quarrelled on route to India and now their menfolk were quarrelling in Serampore. To make matters worse, Grant caught a fever immediately on arriving at Serampore and died after a very brief illness, leaving a widow and two children. Carey could find little comfort from his wife during these trials. At this time, according to Ward's diary, Mrs Carey was 'wholly deranged'.

On the positive side, the Danish Governor of Serampore, Ole Bie, told the British missionaries that they could count on his support. His government, assisted by the Germans, had been supporting Indian missions for over 100 years and he had been converted through the testimony of Christian Friedrich Schwartz (1726-1798) of the Halle and SPCK Mission at Tranquebar. Schwartz was instrumental in leading many Indians to Christ and founded a number of indigenous churches and schools in Tamil and Hindi speaking regions. At Tranquebar and Madras, Bibles had been printed in Tamil, Telugi and Hindustani and Bie wanted the same blessing for the Bengalis. So the Governor now asked the British missionaries to help him establish a church, printing press and schools in Serampore. Hearing that Ward and his fellow-missionaries needed Carey's advice on how they should proceed, Governor Bie angered the British by fitting Ward out with a Danish passport so that he could move through British controlled territory and visit Carey. Through Ward, Carey was told that the Danish government would allow them to found schools, translate the Scriptures and preach with no let or hindrance. Furthermore, the Christian governor would fit all the British missionaries out with Danish passports which would also give them protection in British districts. Very soon, Britain would declare war on the Danish settlements in India. Ostensibly, the reason given was Denmark's friendship with France. However, Denmark's policy of supporting the evangelizing of the Indians had become a thorn in the flesh to the British and it was obvious the missionary question which increased their hatred of the Danes. Indeed King Frederick of Denmark, who supported Indian missions and corresponded personally with Carey, Ward and Marshman, told them later that during the troubles with Britain, he had refused to surrender Serampore because, in 1801, he had personally promised the missionaries protection and refused to break his word. For him, the giving up of Serampore would have meant the end of the gospel in India. Protesting strongly at the British East India Company's inhuman policies in India, Cowper wrote to William Unwin who had the ear of William Wilberforce in Parliament:

"... they...have possessed themselves of an immense territory, which they have ruled with a rod of Iron, to which it is impossible they should ever have a right, unless such an one as it is a disgrace to plead, the right of conquest. The Potentates of this Country they dash in pieces like a potter's vessel as often as they please, making the happiness of 30 millions of mankind a consideration subordinate to that of their own emolument, oppressing them as often as it may serve a lucrative purpose, and in no instance have I heard, consulting their interest or advantage."[80]

Not all the British East Indian officials were anti-missionary. Many had not forgotten that at the birth of the Company in 1600, the spreading of the gospel in India had been one of its major aims. Company Director Charles Grant had been campaigning for missionaries to India since 1787, encouraging Anglicans and Baptists alike to put their hand to the foreign plough. However, he found himself powerless even to obtain passports for the British missionaries and advised them to remain under Danish protection. He supported the mission financially, bought Kiernander's church building for their use after the Swede died and left a substantial legacy for them at his own death. David Brown, an English chaplain to the East India Company, in spite of his strong distrust of Thomas, sought to help Carey and his friends as much as possible by mediating between them, the police office and the East Indian officials. He, and several other non-Baptist supporters, would have become communicants at the mission church in 1800 according to the wishes of Cary, Marshman and Ward but for Fuller's opposition who denied that these field-workers were 'real Christians'. In these early years, however, Christians of various denominational backgrounds made up the bulk of Carey's fellow-worshippers as his sound preaching and teaching had moved them to find fellowship with him. Exclusive communion had not been the practice of the earlier generations of Particular Baptists. Andrew Fuller had nothing against begging non-Baptists to finance

---

[80] *Letters and Prose Writings*, II, 195.

the East India Mission, or give them political support, but he would not have them partake of 'the cup of blessing' in the churches they had helped to established and in the church buildings they had provided or even erected. Indeed, Fuller told the Serampore Trio, as they came to be known, that their idea smacked of the Anti-Christ and fellowshipping with non-Baptists at the Table was like opening the doors to immorality and dangerous heresy. When this news spread around, Fuller defended his interference in the work at Serampore in the Christian press by stating that it was not a question of open or closed communion but of the validity of being a Baptist. For a Baptist to fellowship with Anglicans and Presbyterians would mean he was no longer a Baptist. So the group of fine, eager Christians at Serampore, some of whom had been converted through Carey's ministry, could not establish a true church as desired but had to opt for an exclusive denomination. Ward tells us that the missionaries to India followed Fuller's ruling most regrettably so as not to 'rock the boat' and cause an open breech between the Society and the East India Mission. However, though the London Missionary Society was of great assistance to the Baptists and such as Forsyth at Calcutta hoped for a joint missionary approach with them, inter-communion between the two societies was now made impossible and the missionaries were no longer pulling on the same rope. Oddly enough, Fuller did not protest at the fact that the British missionaries were gradually coming under the financial and organisational influence of Danish Lutherans who, nevertheless, shared their intense desire to win the Indians for Christ as much as did many Anglicans and a growing number of Presbyterians. Indeed, American Presbyterians such as Captain Wickes were now also supporting the mission. Adoniram Judson was originally sent out to assist Carey as a Presbyterian missionary. Carey expert, Professor Bengt Sundkler, of Uppsala University, a fervent evangelical but hater of blind denominationalism, wrote a fine book showing how William Carey was the father of true, Biblical oecumenicity. He much regretted the fact that influential believers had failed to rally around him because of their denominational prejudice and the oecumenical movement thus fell into the hands of worldly churches who nevertheless hail Carey as their father.

The move to Serampore

When Ward reached Carey, still holding out at the Mudnabati factory, he pleaded with him to move to Serampore. There was no hope for the immediate furtherance of the gospel in British India, he argued, but in Serampore they could preach and teach freely and could print the Bengali Bible. Besides, the area around Serampore was densely populated and the Danes were anxious that more missionaries should join them. Carey was in a real dilemma as he had grown to love Mudnabati and had invested £500 in his property there. Nevertheless, he realised that Ward's advice was sound, so he packed up and moved to Serampore, taking up his residence there on 10th January 1800. The day after he was presented to his sponsor and protector Governor Bie after which he went out and preached to the Indians. George Smith writes that Carey's apprenticeship was now over and he had begun his full apostolate.

Carey had arrived in Serampore just in time. Soon after, British troops stormed Serampore without any opposition from the surprised Danes who had not dreamt that such a breech of international diplomacy could occur. As the British confiscated the Danish East India Companies trading vessels, the Danes realised that it was more their commerce that the British wanted, not their political submission. The Danish King refused to give way to the British who had to wait until 1845 before they could take over the more or less besieged enclave 'legally'. Meanwhile, the mission prospered and spread. Carey was given the most prominent building in the city for the church in which he preached for the next thirty-four years. The town of Serampore, too, prospered as it proved an asylum of peace for fugitives from the Americo-Franco-British wars and it persuaded many wealthy investors to settle there. More missionaries were urgently needed as Brunsdon soon died of a liver complaint. Fountain, who was doing pioneer work at Dinapoor, also died after a short illness. Thomas rejoined the mission at Serampore but was also soon called home. George Smith claims that Fountain and Thomas had been mistakes, probably thinking of Fountain's republican politics and Thomas's erratic life. The latter, however, had been most successful as a preacher and had often urged the Baptist missionary movement on to new activity when they felt most discouraged. So, too, the mission's first converts were through Thomas' preaching and fatherly care for his patients so it would be most wrong to rob Thomas of the privilege of being regarded as a great pioneer of the Baptist East India Mission. Fountain was an ideal missionary and there were many Republicans amongst the British Baptists at the time and a greater number who sided with America and sympathised with France during those disastrous late eighteenth and early nineteenth century wars. All the Americans who identified themselves with Carey were Republicans, but no less useful as missionaries for that.

The missionaries were able to purchase a very large house in the middle of the town with two acres of garden from the Governor's nephew for £800. This amounted to a mere four years' rent. Ward wrote, "The price alarmed us, but we had no alternative; and we hope that this will form a comfortable missionary settlement. Being near Calcutta, it is of the utmost importance to our school, our press, and our connection with England.' In no time, Ward had set up his press, sufficient paper was at hand and he began to print the Bengali Bible. Due to the generosity of the Danish King, the missionaries were able to add a school, a college, a hostel and private houses so that within a few years, the buildings alone of the mission station covered five acres. These were set in several acres of botanical gardens. Soon after settling in Serampore, Carey realised what a godsend Ward and Marshman were. He told the Society, "Brother Ward is the very man we wanted: he enters into the work with his whole soul. I have much pleasure in him, and expect much from him. Brother Marshman is a prodigy of diligence and prudence, as in also his wife in the latter: learning the language is mere play to him; he has already acquired as much as I did in double the time." Ward had more difficulties with language learning but Carey found him, 'so holy, so spiritual a man' and he soon became a favourite of the Indian children. The missionaries drew up an order of family rules, regulating who prayed and led the worship at what times, who took care of the common purse, who looked after the medical equipment and who took care of the library. All business and trade that was done was jointly regulated by the missionaries who now called themselves 'the Family'. The British Baptists had seen this work in their predecessors the Moravians and found that it worked with them equally well. Marshman wrote, "Thank you, Moravians. If ever I am a missionary worth a straw, I shall owe it, under God, to you." Knowing human nature, it is sheer miracle that these men and women were able to live in near absolute harmony though their day was organised so that little or no private family leisure was possible.

The mission prospers

In 1789 Fuller had promised the Indian mission £360 per annum. Though this was a vain promise, it does appear that the Society had paid a substantial contribution to the Serampore work which challenged Carey's ideas of independence somewhat. Happily, the printing of the Bengali Bible now went ahead at full speed and with the income from the press and the schools alone, the missionary family became 'more than self supporting'. So, after a further year and in order to set the Serampore mission on its own feet, they started to pay back the money they had hitherto received from the Society, the entire amount being returned within five years. Further building projects were financed by the mission itself, with the added assistance of friends in India. The mission now owned property valued at several thousand pounds, but so strong was the desire amongst the missionaries not to make any personal profit from their now lucrative real estate that they signed over all the Serampore Mission rights and assets to date to the Society. This was eventually altered to allow the missionaries a tenth of their profits in order to make provisions for widows and orphans. This meant that the East Indian Mission was now one of the Society's major financial supporters. The Serampore Mission was no longer the proprietors of their own property but retained much of the trusteeship. Hand in hand with their principles which had brought material progress, Carey prayed, "If we are enabled to preserve in the same principles, we may hope that multitudes of converted souls will have reason to bless God to all eternity for sending the Gospel into this country." Though Carey's biographers could now testify to the palatial circumstances under which the missionaries lived, they could also testify to the great harvest of souls the missionaries now began to reap.

Already towards the end of 1800, a few Indians had begun to profess Christ. The first who offered himself for baptism, a man named Fakira, soon fell by the wayside under the pressure of his family. Krishna Pal, however, a former guru, now recognised the burden of his sins and, after calling Thomas to attend to his dislocated shoulder, found Christ as his Saviour as the doctor-missionary attended to his injuries and spoke to his troubled heart. Whenever Krishna Pal attended the mission house to receive treatment, he was also built up in the faith through young Felix Carey's and Ward's ministry. Krishna Pal was instrumental in having his wife; his four daughters; his wife's family and several other Hindoos follow him to Christ and formed the first Indian church north of Madras. Krishna Pal became an accomplished speaker and hymn writer and Carey's tutor in various dialects. There is a beautiful letter extant in Krishna Pal's hand, dated 12th October, 1800 testifying to the great change Christ had made in his life. On 29th December Carey wrote: "Yesterday was a day of great joy. I had the happiness to desecrate the Gunga (River), by baptising the first Hindoo, viz. Krishna, and my son Felix." In many ways, however, Krishna's baptism was a matter for sorrow. Thomas' joy and praise at being instrumental in converting the first Bengalis made him so elated that he lost his mind, became raving mad, and had to be kept behind locked doors during the baptism service. Mrs Carey was also thought too insane to witness the baptism of her son.

Abandoning the practice of the previous British churches who kept to the caste system and even used different cups for different castes at the communion service, the Serampore Trio announced that their worship was to be caste-free. This angered many of the Europeans and the Bengalis themselves demanded that the Indian Christians should be severely punished. The Governor had to come to their rescue as the crowds were crying 'Feringhi'[81] at the newly converted Indians and protesting that the Europeans were striving to rob them of their status as Indians. Governor Bie's assurance that Krishna and his friends had truly become Christians but not Europeans, failed to calm the enraged mob. Nevertheless, the flood-gates had opened and soon many Indians were moved to follow Christ. A fortnight later Jaymani, the first of many Bengali women was baptised, followed soon later by her sister Rasmayi, a leather worker's widow named Annada and a man called Gokool, who had been converted about the same time as Krishna, was baptised with his wife. Then high caste Petumber Singh, who had sought forgiveness of sin for many years, professed Christ, followed by other high caste Indians such as Syam Dass, Petumber Mitter and his wife Draupadi. These were learned people who soon became teachers and preachers to their people. Then Muslims such as Peroo and Brahmins such as Krishna Prosad became Christians, so that within four years, forty native Indians were converted and eight from other stock. A number of these were trained as missionaries to spread the good tidings in other areas and the mission was able to provide them with a small salary.

This turn of events was greatly assisted by the publication of the Bengali New Testament which was first placed on the communion table at Serampore on 5 March, 1801. This academic feat brought the mission to the notice of the King of England who began to take the side of the mission in her dealings with the East India Company. When the complaint went up that such a translation was done without the approval of the East India Company, the King replied that the task of spreading the Scriptures was outside of their jurisdiction and that he was greatly pleased that his subjects were employed in such a manner. Many now claimed that the printing of the first Bengali New Testament was the first step in turning the Indians from their erroneous superstitions. This was only half of the truth. In the providence of God, this first major translation by the British missionaries also helped to turn the British East Indian Company from their erroneous, superstitious attitude towards the citizens of Indian.

---

[81] Portugese for *foreigner*.

Part Four: The Serampore Trio Triumph over Opposition from the Home Front

A wise decision

It was general practice amongst missionary societies to give 'Christian names' to their non-European converts as a demonstration that they had started new lives. This caused the present author great difficulties when tracing the 18th-19th century history of the Baptist mission to the Native American Indians for his book *Isaac McCoy: Apostle of the Western Trail*. He found so many Indians called John Gill, John Calvin or Isaac McCoy in the Southern states and Andrew Fuller in the North that it became impossible to determine if they were the same people as those called Hajekathake, Pos-sa-che-haw, Nam-pa-war-rah or Sa-mau-kau before their baptisms. Once in India, Carey decided to break with this custom and refused to compel the Mission's converts to give up their birth names. This was a wise move as the families of Indian believers looked upon the giving of foreign names to their dear ones as a form of apartheid, separating one family member from another. The rumour even spread that Indians with English 'Christian' names lost their right to be considered Indians and would be deported to England. Sadly, Carey's successors reintroduced the most undiplomatic practice.

Carey's decision not to give converts English or 'biblical' names caused little opposition but when more and more Indian Christians, with Carey's full approval, publicly gave up their castes, protests grew amongst both the Europeans and the Indians. Former Brahmins, Muslims and the casteless who were now Christians sought to convince their fellow-Indians that though they had been taught to look on the outer caste of a person, God looked on their hearts and thus castes were of no account whatsoever. Thus, when casteless Gokool died, his coffin was carried by Bhyrub, a converted Brahmin and Piru, a former Muslim; besides Marshman and Felix Carey to demonstrate that they were all now one in Christ. So, too, in 1802, Krishna's Christian daughter, a Sudra, was married to a Brahmin convert, the first Christian marriage to occur in North India. A special service was devised for the occasion based on the Church of England rite.

Early blunders

Two of the Mission's new rules for converts, however, proved most controversial; one because of its foolishness and the other because it questioned the traditional Christian and natural views of marriage. The lesser blunder was to give those who offered themselves for baptism six shillings each to encourage them in their stand. This was, for obvious reasons, soon discontinued. Far more questionable was the Society's attitude to marriage. The Mission aimed at converting whole families and the first male converts brought their wives and families into the fold of the church. Soon, however, both men and women were converted whose spouses refused to follow them into the baptismal waters and opposed the gospel. The missionaries prayed weekly all through 1803 for a solution to this major problem but found none. Finally and with hindsight unwisely, they referred the matter to the Society and Andrew Fuller responded as the Society's spokesman. He believed that marriages 'outside the Lord' were null and void and a Christian was thus not bound in wedlock by either an unbelieving husband or wife. According to George Smith, Fuller therefore advised the Mission that converted Indians should do all in their power to have their spouses worship with them but if this proved impossible after a reasonable period of time, they should divorce their spouses and be free to remarry. Such Christian divorcees could then take up church offices. Oddly enough, those who had several wives were not asked to divorce any of them but were merely not allowed to become office-bearers in the Church. The Baptist Society's advice ignored the fact that marriage was a natural creation act and love, care, devotion and faithfulness played a large role in maintaining marriage bonds, whatever the religion of the participants was. The Dissenting churches of Commonwealth times and the Church of England at the Restoration had equally stressed that marriage was a civil contract. The two who became one flesh were therefore not necessarily Christians. Marriage was for a Cain as well as an Abel; an Esau as well as a Jacob. One could not force a Christian to divorce on the grounds that he or she had married whilst unconverted. In the early days of the Baptists, marriage 'outside of the congregation' was, according to J. J. Goadby, either not recognised as 'legal' or led to excommunication. A Christian could thus be excommunicated for refusing to desert his wife. This was certainly not the intention of the New Testament writers on divorce. Be this as it may, within the next few years, Carey and his friends had won many converts amongst the Europeans, Asians, Eurasians and some hundred Indians were now staunch Christians. Church buildings were being raised which would have been the pride of any British church of whatever denomination. Many Indians were marrying 'in the Lord' and founding Christian families. The Serampore Trio's work was thoroughly successful.

Professor Carey

The East Indian Company was now absorbed into the British Empire and in 1800, Lord Wellesley, the Governor-General, founded Fort William College at Calcutta for the instruction of imperial civil servants. Chaplain David Brown, a faithful and energetic Anglican supporter of the Mission, was chosen by Wellesley as Provost. Brilliant scholars were appointed for the various posts and Brown insisted that Carey was the man most fitted to become Professor of Bengali as he had shown his academic abilities in his translation work and other linguistic studies. Carey accepted the post and immediately received an enormous salary which was doubled after a very short period. Carey was now earning £1,500 per annum which was ten times that of a normal English pastor. Furthermore, Carey was asked to found a department for the translation of Scripture into Indian languages. Thus, though foreign missionaries were refused entrance into British Bengal for a number of years and missionaries already there were severely hindered in their work, Carey could engage Marshman and Wade in the provision of grammars, text books and translations from the Classics and Scripture for the further education of Eton scholars and the Anglo-Indian aristocracy. Carey was one of only two Europeans who could speak and write Sanskrit as well as the most learned Brahmins, so almost immediately, he was also given a professorship in Sanskrit and was able to find posts for a number of his better educated Indian converts. Over the years, he was able to build up a library of the greatest works in Sanskrit and other ancient and modern Indian and Asian languages, the bulk of these books being still available to scholars behind fire-proof doors in the Regent's Park College Library. For anyone hoping to do missionary work in India or academic work in the ancient Indian languages, a prolonged visit to Regent's Park College Library is an absolute must. Carey, a workaholic if ever there was one, took all the tasks of a professor in his stride and still found time to preach and teach the gospel several days a week amongst the Indians. He was also able to found and preside over an Indian training college at Serampore for future pastors and teachers.

The Society demands sole authority over the Indian Mission's Funds and Property

The Serampore Trio invested nine-tenths of their large income in worldwide missions. The rest was used for the daily needs of the growing missionary family. Carey's mission was thus the greatest financial supporter of the British Baptist Missionary Society worldwide. The figures speak for themselves. During Carey's forty years in India, he personally received a mere £600 from the home committee. On the other hand, Carey donated most of the £46,000 he earned as a business man and Professor in India to the Society's work. The other missionaries doubled this amount between them and their non-Society friends in India provided another £80,000. Rather than rejoice at this situation, the sad truth is that the more Carey's Mission became totally self-supporting and expansive, the more the Society wished to have full control over all its financial resources, including the major amount of property provided by non-Baptist Christian friends and the Danish royal family and diplomats. Furthermore, the Society wished to have full control over the personal lives and agendas of the missionaries. They demanded a fully transparent East Indian Mission, with themselves as 'Big Brother' watching over and administrating it. The Serampore Trio wisely saw that the Society was totally lacking in the acumen and experience needed to rule the East India Mission from afar and that Fuller and his associates could not understand the needs of India. Thus, when Fuller and the home committee strove to govern the Serampore Church like absentee vicars, they hampered the Mission's work greatly and dropped the rope they had promised to hold in support of Carey. When Fuller died in 1815, the remaining founders and the new Committee became even more antagonistic towards the Serampore missionary strategy and evangelistic outreach. Indeed, they now complained that the Serampore Trio were making themselves rich at the expense of the Mission and treated them with great suspicion as if they were fiddling the Society's books. They became so grasping that Carey threatened to give them all the assets of the Indian Mission and go off and found another mission, run by those at the Indian front alone.

The Society did not reveal the true circumstances of the East Indian Mission to the general public as it would have been detrimental to their fund raising. India was certainly the country which captured the interest of British believers the most so the Society kept on advertising the work in India as their prime target for funds. Thus, people thinking they were contributing to the spread of the gospel in India were actually contributing to the mission elsewhere where the methods of the Society were far less successful, indeed where they were often disastrous and ill-planned. A similar state of affairs in North America prevailed where William Staughton, a co-founder of the British Baptist Mission, was guilty of a most deceitful strategy. Monies canvassed for the spread of the gospel to the Native Americans were used for the world-wide mission and a training college which barred Indians and soon went bankrupt. This scandal brought the American Society to its knees and Isaac McCoy, pioneer missionary to the Native

Americans, who strove to follow in Carey's footsteps, eventually formed a new mission and helped found the Southern Baptist Convention. Staughton was made responsible for American funds in support of Carey's Serampore work but instead of passing them on, he kept them back claiming that Carey's educational policy was false as he had botany and physics taught in Serampore College. This, Staughton agued, was unbecoming for a Christian missionary. The difference between the western 'Indians' and those of the East was that McCoy's 'Indians' suffered greatly because they did not receive funds earmarked for them, whereas Carey's Indians were chiefly aided by the missionaries' own earnings. Such facts quite disprove the teaching of modern Fullerites who would have us believe that Carey and the Home Committee where always of 'one heart and one soul' and that Carey's success was because he put into practice all that was dictated to him by Staughton, Fuller, Ryland, Hall and company.

Though Carey did not agree with the Society over the financing of the mission and was often tempted to break with them, he believed initially that his influence would be greater within the Baptist Missionary Society than outside of it. When one reviews the accounts of the Society's own fund-raising work soberly, it is clear that the larger donations came from outside of the Committee's denominational circle and that the amounts raised were far too modest to finance a large world-wide mission, not to mention a single mission in India. Two great exceptions were the Society's success in raising over a thousand pounds for Bible Society work and in meeting the costs caused by a fire in the Mission's printing department in India. However, the bulk of these monies came from outside of the denomination and such rare donations were paid back with interest by the Carey Mission. Even when members of Carey's wider 'Missionary Family' were fitted out materially for their pioneer work by the Society, Carey regarded this act as one of mere supply on demand and paid the Society in full.

The Home Society breaks with the Serampore Trio

From 1815 to 1820, Carey gradually realised that the Society was systematically striving to hinder his work in India and destroy his missionary ideals. They had begun to send out very young inexperienced, albeit gifted, men in their early twenties who were told not to join the Serampore Trio's 'Family' and take their orders directly from the Home Committee. They would be salaried directly from England and there was to be no pooling of income. Ignoring the great pioneer work of Carey, Wade and Marshman, these greenhorns started up a work of their own under the name of 'Calcutta Missionary Union', professing to be the 'real' British Baptist Mission in

India. This work included duplicating schools and churches to compete with those of the old mission which was typical of the Society's own chaotic waste of their supporters' good money. Deliberately basing their work in areas where the gospel was already thriving, the newcomers refused to do pioneer work. They were obviously merely 'cashing in' on the Serampore Trio's success. It was not long before some of these untrained youngsters promoted the Liberalism of Fuller, Ryland Jun. and the Halls and erred into Unitarianism. Marshman made a journey to England to sort out the mess but found the Society had lost the missionary zeal present at the time of its foundation. All the old Fullerites, including Robert Hall, were now against them. On arriving back in India after three-years' begging the Society not to rock the boat, Carey wrote that he was shocked to find his fellow-labourer looking fifteen years older.

The 'old mission' was now greatly restricted in their work of expansion as the new missionaries just would not cooperate with them. No wonder Carey wrote, 'I am greatly afflicted' and called the Society's hostile strategy 'a Counter-Baptist Mission'. Again, he protested that he had understood the work of the Society as supporting their brethren on the mission field by 'holding the rope for them' but they had now removed their brethren from the India end of the rope and placed mere Society servants in their place. The Serampore Trio refused to become servile to the incompetent and un-Biblical whims of the Society, yet throughout this period they continued to use their income for the support of the Society's work. The Society, however, claimed that more ought to be forthcoming. Carey replied that he kept so little for his own daily needs that if he were to die on the spot, his widow would not have funds to pay for his funeral. However, Carey told Ryland privately that he refused to take action against the new policies of the Society and would carry on as usual not wishing 'to mortify anyone by proving they were wrong'. Now, even Ryland turned against the missionaries and especially Marshman of whom Carey said 'I wish I had half his piety, energy of mind, and zeal'. Ryland's letters became plainly insulting and the Society poured 'hailstorms of accusations' on Marshman and Carey (William Ward had died in 1823) via the Christian press. Carey's correspondence was now even cut and reshaped by the Society to 'prove' that he had been 'unrighteous' all along. Carey told Ryland that he was acting evilly and regretted that his former brethren now looked on him as a renegade servant of the Society. Now, even members of Carey's family were solicited by the Society to 'squeal on' Carey and Marshman. By March, 1827, Carey and Marshman were officially no longer considered the Society's servants and were cut off from the Society's pseudo-fellowship and support.

Two old men leave the Society to its own folly and continue God's eternal work

Carey and Marshman were too stalwart in character to be put off by such unjust and unworthy action. They alone sought to bridge the great divide which had come between them and the Society. Both were men who scorned riches but were extremely successful in earning money for others in need. In 1830, they now did what they had threatened to do decades before. They signed over the entire Serampore property and income to the English Society's trustees, though, humanly speaking, the Society had no right to it, and merely asked to be able to live rent free with their families for the rest of their lives. The Society responded with glee but divine justice intervened; the Calcutta banks crashed so that the Society was not able to cash in on the revenues from the buildings as hoped. The Serampore work suffered less from the crash as Cary and Marshman were used to attempting great things through their own God-given energies and they had many hundreds of believers in India behind them. So too, both the East India Company and the British Government now viewed Carey most favourably and joined with the Danes in supporting him. So Carey was free to get on with his missionary work without, as he said, the Society wasting his precious time. He continued with making the Scriptures available in various dialects and the last sheet of his new Bengali edition was completed in June 1832. With Lord Hastings as his patron, Carey founded a seaman's mission in Calcutta and purchased a boat to be used as a mobile missionary station. He was even able, though now over seventy years of age, to establish new stations in a number of unevangelised areas. Suddenly, he felt it was now time to hand his mantle to the grand, eager and highly qualified group of youngsters who had kept faithful to the cause of India. Most of these were the children and grandchildren of the pioneer missionaries who had been led by the Serampore Trio. Carey confessed to them that, in his old age, he had 'scarcely a wish ungratified'. On 9 June, 1834 William Carey passed peacefully through death to eternal life. Before his home-call, he asked for a few words from a hymn by Watts to be placed on his grave and nothing more:

A wretched, poor and helpless worm,
On thy kind arms I fall.

The entire history of William Carey is of a man with but one divine ambition who was able, by the grace of God, to accomplish all that he was called to do. That he achieved his goal is all the more astonishing in view of the enormous lack of understanding concerning his theology, missionary strategy and evangelistic fervour shown by the very para-church organisation which had pledged itself to support him but had done its level best to hamper him.

William Carey

"A plodder for Christ", "Father of modern Missions", but, mostly, Bible Translator.

By C. P. Hallihan

C. P. Hallihan – 'Peter' – was born in 1940 in the English Lake District. Brought up in a practicing Roman Catholic family, he abandoned all pretence of religion in his teens. By the grace of God, the Gospel came to him at age twenty-one, bringing salvation through faith in Jesus Christ. Almost from the beginning the burden to preach Christ and open the Scriptures was irresistible. Three years in a Bible school followed, and then forty-one years as pastor of a rural Baptist church in Shropshire and a preaching ministry through many parts of England. Through most of those years there was involvement with the Trinitarian Bible Society, leading to a formal position in the Editorial Department from 1992. Peter is married to Barbara, the both have four children and now four grandchildren.

Reprinted with permission of the Trinitarina Bible Society, London (www.trinitarianbiblesociety.org) from Trinitarian Bible Society Quarterly Record Issue No. 554: Jan – Mar 2001, pp. 7-17

Introduction

The life, times, and ministry of William Carey form an heroic, epic page in the war diaries of the Church Militant here in the earth. His connection with the cause of the Gospel of our Lord Jesus Christ on the Indian subcontinent was briefly touched upon in a recent "country article" in TBS *Quarterly Record* No. 553. The intent now is not to write a "Life of Carey", or "India, part 2", but to focus on Carey's connection with, and impact on, the whole work of Bible Translation, and indeed on the nature of a Bible Society. This, however, cannot be done without at least an outline of the man's life and work.

> "Therefore blessed be they, and most honoured be their name, that break the ice, and give the onset upon that which helpeth forward to the saving of souls. Now what can be more available thereto than to deliver God's people in a tongue which they can understand?"[82]

---

[82] *The Translators to the Reader* (reprint London: Trinitarian Bible Society, 1998), p. 18.

Profile: beginnings

Eldest of five children, William Carey was born at Paulerspury, Northampton, England, on August 17th 1761, when the tide of the Evangelical Awakening was at its flood in the nation. As with some other notable Baptists, Bunyan before him and Spurgeon after, he began in rural obscurity with but an 'ordinary' education. Raised in a nominal connection with the (Anglican) Parish Church, he was remarked on as a youngster for a determination to finish any task, and steadfastly to acquire knowledge. He was also a diligent and thoughtful observer of the world about him. Apprenticed at sixteen to a shoemaker, Carey found the senior apprentice to be that despised thing – a "dissenter" or "non-conformist". Conversation, argument and discussion with the Dissenter brought Carey under the good hand of God to faith in Christ Jesus. He was baptised in the river Nene, near Northampton, by John Ryland, and maintained the connection with Baptists ever after. Seeking, from the beginning, opportunity to preach, he thought best to equip himself for ministry by diligent daily Bible reading and the acquisition of the Biblical Languages as well as Latin, German and French. Much of his Bible study was without formal guidance, but was with assiduous reference to the languages of inspiration. He also responded to the demands of reading the Bible in such other tongues as he knew, which tends to prevent unconscious and unchallenged acceptance of understandings based on the 'accidents' of one's own language. All of this was accomplished while still working at his trades, with books conveniently sited for perusal whilst working. His life-long conviction as to the enduring sufficiency and self-attestation of the Scriptures was grounded here. When Erasmus in the sixteenth century published his New Testament Paraphrases for "women and cobblers, clowns, mechanics, and even the Turks,"[83] he could not have envisaged this torch bearer two centuries afterward, this cobbler, this mechanic, mastered by the Gospel, compelled by the Word, carrying the vernacular Scriptures far beyond the Turks, to the pagans of India. As unwitting prophets, the Baptist Church at Olney called ('licensed') Carey, the shoemaker, schoolmaster, scholar, but, above all, servant of Christ, after some long deliberation and trial of his gifts, to preach 'wherever the providence of God might open his way'.

---

[83] These paraphrases were published over many years, from 1517 onwards, and translated into several European languages. Miles Coverdale superintended the translation of one such into English for Queen Catherine Parr. All Erasmus' editions had statements in the preface similar to the one mentioned above, ringing the changes on 'farmers, travellers, tailors, labourers' etc., but always including the Turks.

Profile: the sending

By connection with local Baptist Association meetings Carey became friendly with Andrew Fuller, and in their fellowship together was formulated a burden for the wider propagation of the Gospel. In 1792 Carey wrote "An enquiry into the obligations of Christians to use means for the Conversion of the Heathen," and in the same year preached a famous sermon, summarised as "Expect great things from God – Attempt great things for God". Historians have compared the sermon with that of Peter on the day of Pentecost in terms of its world-shaking consequences. After a subsequent meeting in October of 1792 the 'Particular Baptist Society for the propagation of the Gospel among the Heathen' was constituted. By the following spring, in his 33rd year, William Carey was en route to India: he had married Dorothy Plackett in 1781, so the transference to India was 'en famille'. Carey was actually sent forth as an assistant to one John (Jack) Thomas, a zealous Christian returning to Bengal. Thomas' inadequacy in money matters reduced the little group to penury, needing employment in an indigo plant to support themselves. Carey's passionate pursuit of knowledge as a young man bore rich practical fruit in such situations, and his ability to bring wisdom to bear on so many matters, from indigo processing to printing house procedures, and later to college administration, should not be lost sight of as providing, in the Providence of our great God, the necessary infrastructure to his greater tasks. The lowly tradesman privately prepared of God soon proved to be the 'Paul' to his companion's 'Barnabas'.

For over forty years in India, William Carey laboured in the Gospel, preaching, preparing translations and publishing them; and then he died, June 1834. His relationship with the British authorities, the slow recognition of his scholarship by the academic establishment, his large contribution in righteousness and equity to the general needs of the population around him, as in his utter resistance of infanticide and the immolation of widows (suttee) cannot be explored here. Even the details of the Serampore College, founded 1818, and the stormy relationship with supporting friends in England must not detain us! The anguished story of his family trials – insanity, bereavement – and the seeming total loss by fire of more than twelve years printing work and equipment, you must seek elsewhere. We must consider Carey in connection with the Bible.

Mission and the Bible

William Carey's understanding of that labour in the Gospel to which he had been so powerfully compelled can be summarised in two points.
- The missionary was to be at one with the people to whom he was to preach.
- The most pressing, demanding, necessity in any new field was the provision of the Scripture in the vernacular, the 'common tongue'.

> "But now what piety without truth? What truth (what saving truth) without the word of God? What word of God (whereof we may be sure) without the Scripture?"[84]

In the first point Carey anticipated as complete a cultural and circumstantial identity with those amongst whom he laboured as righteousness allowed: to settle, and live, and die amongst them, rather than to visit them. The situation, conditions, resources and expectations were ever the same both for evangelised and evangelist, saving only his recourse to the Throne of Grace and confidence in Sovereign Providence. This feature is a challenging aspect of those groundbreaking missionaries, the likes of Judson in Burma, Williams and Paton in the Pacific Islands, W. Chalmers Burns and Griffith John in China, and so many more, who counted identity with those to whom they were called a great enough wealth to set against ostracism by their fellow Europeans. The impact of this concept on the second point should never be underestimated. Carey was utterly convinced that as his own capacity to speak to the population was limited by many factors, not least the appointed span of human life, it was of the utmost importance to bring into the life and language of these people an abiding testimony, the Bible, that would go on 'speaking' long after his scant years, with or without human agency. His capacity to do this was, in the rich provisions of our great God, hugely extended by his identity with those to whom he sought to hold forth the word of life. Carey and his team scarcely viewed Bible Translation as a distinct work accomplished by 'experts', but rather the domestic product of the Missionary, with his converts, in his community; and so they became the 'experts'. It was axiomatic for these men of God that the only possible procedure for securing Bible versions of spiritual worth and enduring quality was to translate from the original languages of inspiration, Hebrew and Greek.

---

[84] *The Translators to the Reader*, p. 10.

Carey's Bibles

Just as the Gospel had been preached, and believed, in India before Carey's arrival, so also there had been Protestant labours of Bible translation into Indian tongues before that time. As early as 1688 a Dutch community in Ceylon had produced a Tamil New Testament. The missionary Schultze made, but never disseminated, a Telugu version around 1730, and later, around 1750, published a Hindi New Testament. These were but the harbingers of the astonishing flood of Bible versions that was now to come from Carey and the Serampore community. Various figures are given as totals of the output, but it seems likely that the number of Scripture versions which Carey directly sent out was twenty-one whole Bibles and seven New Testaments. Beyond that he certainly had a part in the planning and preparation of very many more, as the hand and name of some master painter can be seen in all the work of his 'school'.

> "Translation it is that openeth the window, to let in the light; that breaketh the shell, that we may eat the kernel; that putteth aside the curtain, that we may look into the most holy place; that removeth the cover of the well, that may we come by the water ..."[85]

The Bengali Bible was the first-fruits of Carey's work; a New Testament appeared in 1801, translated directly from Greek, beginning in 1796. Four times Carey revised the manuscript before print, with a Greek Concordance beside him, and in company with Ram Basu, a Bengali scholar (pundit) who had professed Christ under the earlier labours of Jack Thomas. These two worked with continual recourse to as many of the local population, hundreds at times, as would gather to hear, read and comment.[86] Parts of the Testament were printed as soon as ready, and distributed, and it brings a part rueful, part affectionate smile to those here involved with new Bible projects to hear of their discussion as to which of the Gospels should be circulated first.[87] The Serampore friends first issued Matthew, as containing a complete life of the Redeemer. A complete Bengali Testament did for

---

[85] Ibid., p. 12.
[86] Carey early learned that to ask someone to read aloud is the surest way of discerning whether or not they comprehend the meaning of what they read. It is a salutary exercise in any Bible Class!
[87] Each of the Four Gospels has its own fierce advocates as to which should be first for circulation. Some will say why not wait until all is ready, but, as in Carey's time, production practicalities, and the sheer desire to disseminate the Light of Scripture Truth, usually lead to one or other appearing as forerunner to a Testament, then a Bible.

the language what the early Luther versions did for German – it was the fountain head of a literary language. Furthermore, it brought Carey to academic recognition, nothing that he desired for itself, but it wondrously enlarged his sphere of useful acceptance for the burden of his heart touching the multiplication and distribution of the Word of God. When copies of the Bengali Testament reached England, Andrew Fuller directed one to the second Earl Spencer, for the great library at Althorp, Northamptonshire, on which estate Carey had once been a very poor tenant. Earl Spencer not only sent a cheque for £50 towards the expense of producing the Old Testament, but ensured that a copy of the Bengali New Testament be presented to King George III.

Certain writings about Carey mention Scriptures in forty languages and dialects as being the work of his hands. He, in his own times, deprecated such statements as exaggerated, not giving due credit to his fellow labourers, and confusing his editing, proofing and press-work, with the direct work of translation. His own works centred around the chief derivations of Sanskrit. He insisted that Sanskrit was the key, and that his hard wrought mastery in the language gave him a four-fifths grasp of the vocabulary and etymology of the chief languages of India. This was certainly true in philological terms, and he found Ooriya, Orissa, Gujarati, among several others, quickly yielded to his labours in the light of his Sanskrit ability. It was also the only language in which the 'high scholars' of India might condescend to read the Scriptures. For the common people the need was for Hindi. To this day Hindi is the language which binds the people of India in some common understanding. Carey published the Scriptures in Sanskrit in 1809, and in Hindi in 1811. He also mastered the Hindu 'theological' writings, inflaming yet further his longing to communicate the light of Truth to the people. It was his considered opinion that the impractical concepts of physics, medicine, chronology and geography which prevailed in the Indian mind were directly attributable to their idolatry, and inadequate concept of Creation.

Some further glimpse of the great mind of this dear man of God is found in his anxiety to compile as much as possible of his philological and lexical work into published grammars and dictionaries. This was so that those who came after could truly stand on his shoulders, and not lose time covering the same ground again. Oh, and by the way, he also struggled to manufacture a form of paper which was less porous, more resistant to insect attack, better able to keep its appearance, than the local product. A manufactory was begun and production of the paper was subsequently expedited by the use of the very first steam-engine to be erected in India. "Serampore Paper" became known all over India, and its production under that name continued long after any connection with the Mission or Gospel work of Serampore had ended. In among these labours Carey became known for his gentle but firm resistance to any interruption of his Bible work. He has been likened to Jerome, to Ulfilas, to Wyclif, to Luther, but saw himself only as a plodder, and would long for a native born Tyndale to further the work.

Bible Societies

As the Gospel had been preached and the Scriptures translated in India before the times of Carey, so also had there been 'Bible Societies' in existence. In 1780 a Society had been formed to put the English Scriptures into the hands of soldiers and sailors. Local, regional and specific associations for the circulation of the Bible came and went. In that setting the whole association of Carey's helpers in the home country, those who 'held the ropes' whilst he and his colleagues laboured, were necessarily an unformed "Bible society" as well as a proto-Missionary Society. Under the leadership of Fuller and Rylands they corresponded, and sought to encourage, support and even to direct the work. The difficulties, anxieties, suspicions and personal grief for Carey which this connection generated at times is a sad testimony to the susceptibilities of the human heart to Satan's strategic devices to hinder the publication of the Word of God, but we dare not dwell upon it now.

> "... to have the Scriptures in the mother tongue is not a quaint conceit ... but hath been thought upon and put in practice of old, even from the first times of the conversion of any nations; no doubt because it was esteemed most profitable to cause faith to grow in men's hearts the sooner ..."[88]

Many readers will know of the story of Mary Jones, and her foot-weary trek from Llanvihangel to Bala in search of a Welsh Bible to purchase with her slowly earned pennies. The effect of that upon Thomas Charles is, again, well recorded. Less widely realised is that among the gentlemen with whom he conferred in London, leading to the formation of the British and Foreign Bible Society in 1804, were some of Carey's 'rope holders'. Early transactions of that Society carry much reference to and involvement with the work of Carey, his associates, the Serampore College, and the next generation of labourers. When profound differences in matters of principle and procedure brought about a separation and the formation of

---

[88] *The Translators to the Reader*, p. 16.

the Trinitarian Bible Society as distinct from the BFBS in 1831, Carey was still alive! The double ethos of William Carey and Mary Jones shaped the formation of Bible Societies. (Alongside those mentioned, there continued to be many regional and national Societies and Auxiliary Societies formed throughout the nineteenth century.) That double ethos was to hold the ropes and provide support for those best able and situated to accomplish the task of Bible translation, and to provide for the spiritually needy throughout the World, accessible editions of the Bible.

Conclusion

> "... *as the credit of the old books* (he meaneth of the Old Testament) *is to be tried by the Hebrew volumes, so of the New by the Greek tongue*, he meaneth by the original Greek. If truth be to be tried by these tongues, then whence should translation be made, but out of them? These tongues, therefore, (the Scriptures, we say, in those tongues,) we set before us to translate, being the tongues wherein God was pleased to speak to his Church by his Prophets and Apostles."[89]

The work of William Carey in connection with the Bible was securely rooted in his confidence as to the nature of Scripture. The Scriptures, by the Spirit of God, communicate their own authority, integrity and sufficiency: his task under God was to communicate the Scriptures! That he did this by preaching as well as publishing is beyond question, but it is that assured confidence in the Bible, the Word of God, quick and powerful, accomplishing that which the LORD pleases, to which I would direct your thought. Throughout this article there are boxed quotes from the extended introduction to the Authorised Version, "The Translators to the Reader", because I am persuaded that they reflect the same view of the power, part, place and profit of the vernacular Scriptures as Carey's, and indeed, that of the TBS. That this self-attestation of Scripture is best served by a simple dependence upon the original languages as the basis of translation is another continuity of conviction and practice that I perceive in common from AV to Carey to TBS. That those best fitted to do the work of translation are those 'in the field' is implicit in Carey's work and explicit in the procedures of TBS. That the best role for a Bible Society is as "rope holders", supplying all possible help to those manifestly called and equipped to do the work of translation sits as well in the present TBS as in early Serampore. That such help reaches to the physical, practical production of the finished Scriptures in the most suitable way (don't forget his labours with pa-

---

[89] Jerome, *ad Lucininum, Dist. 9., ut veterum*, in Ibid., p. 25.

per and print), and their wide distribution is a point which would secure the vote both of William Carey and the supporters of the TBS. That there is great need for servants of such gifts and calling to be thrust forth into the needy field of these present times is matter that I can only commend to your prayers, and equally to your thankfulness before the Lord; for He does continue to raise up those equipped in the Biblical Languages, burdened for the needs of their Mother Tongue, and sharing the convictions and principles of this Society, so that there are some thirty projects in hand at this time!

> "a blessed thing it is, and will bring us to everlasting blessedness in the end, when God speaketh to us, to hearken; when He setteth His Word before us, to read it ..."[90]

Life of William Carey, Shoemaker & Missionary by George Smith C.I.E., LL.D. First issue of this edition 1909, reprinted 1913, 1922. Although I have given no direct quotations from this source, it has been of great help, with fascinating appendices and footnotes. It is in the public domain, available on the Internet, biblebelievers.com/carey/index.html, but beware – as hard copy it runs out to 70 double-column pages of a 9-point typeface!

---

[90] Ibid., p. 28.

India: Perils and Promise Then And Now

By Vishal Mangalwadi

Vishal Mangalwadi (*1949) is an international lecturer, social reformer, author of thirteen books, and political columnist whom Christianity Today has called "India's foremost Christian intellectual". Mangalwadi specializes in philosophical and political issues. Born and raised in India, Mangalwadi studied under Francis Schaeffer at L'Abri Fellowship in Switzerland.
Mangalwadi, the winner of the Dr. Bhimrao Ambedkar Distinguished National Service Award, writes with a prophetic heart and scholar's mind. He studied philosophy in secular universities, Hindu ashrams and in L'Abri Fellowship before moving into a village in Madhya Pradesh. With his wife Ruth, he founded the Association for Comprehensive Rural Assistance to serve India's poor. From social work, he moved to political activism and served in the headquarters of two national political parties, organizing peasants and the "lower castes."
For some time now he has worked as a free-lance writer and speaker, lecturing to illiterate peasants in India, as well as to university audiences. He loves simplifying complex ideas while firing despairing hearts with hope.
Mangalwadi's other books include *The World of Gurus, Truth and Social Reform* and *Missionary Conspiracy: Letters to a Postmodern Hindu*. He has written a political column for the Dubai-based magazine *The International Indian*.

With kind permission by the editor Chuck Stetson reprinted from Chuck Stetson (ed.). Creating a Better Hour: Lessons from William Wilberforce. Stroud & Hall Publ., Macon (GA), USA, 2007, chapter 9, pp. 135-149.

India is hot today. Huge sums and private equity is now pouring into India because it is a land of great promise: the world's largest democracy with 1.1 billion consumers and a large, educated, English speaking, low-cost work force. Yet, this is not the first time India has appeared as a land of promise. The British East India Company established its first permanent base in India in 1612. It saw the possibilities as early as the 17th century, but by 1757 it found itself trapped in a quagmire. The merchants turned into colonial masters. It took 190 years for the British to extricate themselves from India. Ultimately, the price of India's independence (1947) was a million Hindus, Muslims, and Sikhs dead and ten million made homeless. That is an unpleasant saga: Its edifying feature is the story of the reformers: initially the British – Charles Grant, William Carey, and William Wilberforce – and eventually the Indians from Rammohum Roy to Mahatma Gandhi.

Thanks to the British and Indian reformers, India is no longer as the British had found it. Yet, that Saga teaches us that it is unwise to look only at the promise and ignore the perils. To the shareholders of the East India Company, the only thing that mattered was the profit. In contrast, the reformers also looked at the challenges. They struggled to bless India by changing both India as well as the British Empire.

Two men trumpeted the bugle for reforming India in 1792: Charles Grant (1746-1823) and William Carey (1761-1834). Grant had served in India and seen both the corruption of the British Company as well as the quagmire that was India. His *Observations* on the state of Britain's Asiatic Subjects was written to help his friend, the Evangelical Member of Parliament, William Wilberforce, to transform the very charter of the East India Company. For this reason, Grant's book circulated as a manuscript for a few years before it was printed. Carey, in contrast, published a general *Inquiry* whether all Christians at all times were obliged to follow the Christ's Great Commission to disciple all nations. If the Great Commission was still binding, then was it proper for the British Church to leave nations such as India at the mercy of unscrupulous merchants and soldiers? Shouldn't the Church be sending out missionaries as linguists, educators, and agents of socio-spiritual transformation?

Together, the two books with help from men such as Wilberforce won the argument that Britain must not see India merely as a territory to be exploited for economic gains. Britain must manage India as a steward of India's real sovereign – the almighty Creator. Today's India is a product of the battle these men initiated.

Human Waste Then

In 1793, three years after Charles Grant returned from India to England, William Carey left England to serve as a Christian missionary in India. He found, among other things, wide spread oppression and humans treated as waste and without dignity. He was horrified by the treatment of untouchables, leprosy patients, children and women – specifically through infanticide, child marriage, polygamy, widowhood, widow-burning (sati) and lack of education.

Infanticide

The practice of exposing infants to death was a widespread religious custom, which still exists today, though often supplemented by abortions of female fetuses. Back then, if an infant was sick, it was supposed that the infant was under the influence of an evil spirit. The infant was put into a basket and hung up for three days. Only if the child survived were means then used to save the infant's life. Every winter, children were pushed down into mud-banks in the sea to be either drowned or devoured by crocodiles, all in the fulfillment of the vows that their mothers had made. This was looked upon as a most holy sacrifice – giving the Mother Ganges the fruit of their bodies for the sins of their souls.

Child Marriage

To guard a young girl's safety and to uphold her family's honor, getting her married off at the earliest possible age was considered the best safeguard. Childhood was thus denied to a girl. She was to pass into motherhood before she had time to grow as a person.

The last census of the nineteenth century in Bengal, India revealed that, in and around Calcutta alone, there were ten thousand widows under the age of four and more than fifty thousand between the ages of five and nine. All these child widows were victims of child marriages.

Polygamy

Polygamy was a common practice. Sometimes fifty women were given to one Brahmin man so that their families could boast that they were allied by marriage to a high caste.

Widowhood

When the much older husbands died, their widows were subjected to a terrible plight because they were perceived as bad omens who had brought about the death of their husbands. It was believed that a widow had "eaten her husband". One possibility was to live in widowhood without remarriage. But the widow was looked upon not as a precious individual in need of support to start a new life but as an economic liability. Her parents had already given the bride-price (dowry); the in-laws were not willing to part with their "possessions" and return the dowry to get the young woman remarried. And, of course, the illiterate widow was in no position to earn and become an economic asset for a family.

To add insult to injury, the bereaved widow had to shave off her hair, remove all jewelry and wear white, all to avoid attracting the other men in the family and causing them to go astray. She had to be kept indoors to keep her chaste. Often widows were required to cohabit with the brother-in-law or another male relative for the purpose of producing a son to offer religious obligations for the deceased husband if he had no sons of his own to undertake this important religious rite.

Widow burning

The other option for a widow was to be burned with her dead husband in a ritual known as Sati. Many widows preferred a speedy death to the known and unknown life-long horrors of widowhood. They were deluded into thinking that the act of self-sacrifice would bestow celebrity status on the family and would take seven generations of their family, before and after them, to heaven. They were assured that the heroic act of self-immolation would deify them.

Female Education

Most men were illiterate and, as a rule, all lower caste men and all women were prohibited from studying. A Hindu father enlightened a missionary with his thoughts on education:

> You may educate my sons, and open to them all the stores of knowledge: But my daughters you must not approach, however benevolent your designs. Their ignorance and seclusion are necessary to the honor of my family; a consideration of far greater moment with me than any mental cultivation of which I cannot estimate the benefit. They must be married at an age when your plans of education could scarcely commence.

South-Asia's Linguistic Revolution

Carey recognized that the Indian sub-continent could not be reformed unless the people were educated in the knowledge of truth in their own languages. Pali, the sacred language of Buddhist scriptures had been dead for almost a thousand years. The living literary languages were Sanskrit, Persian, and Arabic. But neither the Brahmin Pandits nor the Muslim Maulvies had a religious or secular motivation to turn the oral dialects of the people into literary languages and to translate their sacred literature into vernaculars. Therefore, Carey began the tedious task of translating the Bible into Indian vernaculars and developing their scripts, grammar etc. Along with some protégés of Charles Grant he raised up a whole team of linguists and translators in Calcutta who created the national languages of modern India (Hindi), Pakistan (Urdu) and Bangladesh (Bengali).

Changing India for the Better

Carey's effort was heroic given the fact that he went to serve India in defiance of the British Parliament only months after it voted against Wilberforce's resolution that the East India Company must allow missionaries to serve India. Since Carey came to British India illegally, he was a fugitive and had to live in the Danish settlement of Serampore. He was welcomed in British India only when the East India Company needed a teacher in Calcutta to teach Bengali at Fort William College. William Carey was hired as an Associate Professor and taught for 30 years, using his position to change India.

Before Charles Grant became a Member of Parliament, William Wilberforce was his spokesman, forcefully arguing in 1793 that England must assume the responsibilities of "uplifting" India. Wilberforce invited Grant to become a fellow resident of Clapham and supported his campaign to become a Director of the East India Company, and eventually a Member of Parliament. Grant believed that besides the corruption of the British Company, the chief problem of India's people was immorality and superstition in the guise of religion. Therefore, education – including moral education and religious re-education – had to be integral aspects of solutions. Good Chaplains were needed to meet the religious needs of the Company staff and missionary educators were needed to open the minds of India's masses. Everyone acknowledged that religious superstitions were terrible opium, yet the Company did not want missionaries to disturb the then existing religious tranquility.

However, by the early 19th century, the doctrine of religious liberty had already come to have two implications. One was that the power of the state should not be used to tamper with the religious conscience of the people. If a social evil such as untouchability or destructive superstitions such as astrology had overt religious sanction, the state could not and should not erase them by mere force or legislation.

The other implication of the doctrine of religious liberty was that the removal of these religiously sanctioned evils had to be the work of counter-reforming religious or nonreligious idea. Therefore, all ideas had to be given the freedom to compete in the marketplace of ideas to change people's beliefs and, thereby, their society.

Wilberforce argued that England should send missionary educators who could help "improve" Indian society. In 1793, he succeeded in pushing his proposals through the House of Commons, but unfortunately, the House of Lords under the influence of the Directors of the East India Company overthrew his proposals. In spite of this official rejection, Carey's sense of a divine call gave him the inner strength to set out for India in the same year.

It took twenty years of successful field work by Carey and his fellow-missionaries in India, lobbying within the East India Company by Charles Grant, and magnificent political work by Wilberforce, to persuade the Parliament to assume its moral obligation to India. In 1813, when the Company's Charter came up for renewal, Wilberforce, once again took up the challenge of transforming the Company's mission in India. This time his crusade was backed by the documentation supplied by Carey and others. These facts included lists of widows who had committed sati. Wilberforce had made a practice of reading their names at his dining table and praying for India. On July 1st and 12th, 1813, Wilberforce argued:

> Let us endeavor to strike our roots into the soil by the gradual introduction and establishment of our own principles and opinions; of our laws, institutions, and manners; above all, as the source of every other improvement, of our religion, and consequently of our morals.

Wilberforce said that such a reforming effort, and not brute military force or political intrigue, would tie India to England with bonds of eternal gratitude.

The critics suggested that, through his advocacy of allowing missionaries to propagate Christianity in India, Wilberforce was counseling compulsory conversion. He rebutted the charge:

> Compulsion and Christianity! Why the very terms are at variance with each other –the ideas are incompatible. In the language of Inspiration itself, Christianity has been called the "law of liberty".

In those days many people in Britain believed that it was necessary to freely dialogue and debate truth. Freedom of conscience was incomplete without the freedom to change one's beliefs, to convert. A state that hinders conversion was considered uncivilized because it restricted human quest for truth and religion.

In politics, however, arguments alone are rarely enough. Wilberforce's proposals regarding India had already been defeated in Parliament more than once. Therefore, in 1813, he took the precaution of mobilizing public pressure, particularly on the House of Lords. The unsuspecting Lords were swept off their feet by the strength of public opinion. The public opinion on which Wilberforce capitalized, was substantially a result of the publicity Carey's work had generated in England during the previous two decades. Today's commitment to pluralism and relativism would condemn

Carey's effort to ban "religious" practices such as Sati and Untouchability; however, back then his work received positive publicity because the intellectual climate was shaped by books written by Grant, Carey, and Claudius Buchanan – *The Christian Researches in Asia* – which gave a vivid first hand account of the horrors of Indian society.

For India, Wilberforce's parliamentary victory had two immediate positive results: a) the East India Company had to allow missionaries freedom to work; and b) the Company was asked to earmark Rs. 100,000 annually from its profits for public education in India. The consequence of the former was that great missionary educators such as Alexander Duff could freely come to India and open schools and colleges. It took twenty additional years of struggle to the next renewal of the Company's charter in 1833 before the reformers' viewpoint really began to determine British policy. The men who spearheaded the 1833 campaign for reforms were Charles Grant, Jr. and Lord Macauly – both sons of the Clapham Sect.

William Carey's efforts

William Carey, as the first missionary, addressed the issues of human waste that he found.

First, the British Governor asked Carey to inquire into the nature and reasons for infanticide. Carey's report resulted in the practice being outlawed.

Second, Carey began to undermine the moral roots of child marriage through the teaching of the Bible and its social roots through female education. It took more than a century of sustained campaign for the practice to be made illegal in 1929 through the Child Marriages Restraint Act. Unfortunately, for many Indians, it is only a "paper legislation." Even Cabinet Ministers in some states in India still marry off their underage daughters.

Third, Carey began to help widows remarry – especially if they had become Christians. That small beginning ultimately resulted in the Widow Remarriage Act of 1856. The law over-ruled religious culture and for the first time, it became right for a Hindu widow to remarry. Until then the only options, especially for a high caste Hindu widow was to suffer lifelong indignity and hardship or commit sati.

Fourth, Carey began his famous campaign against Sati after his horrible, first hand experience in 1799. He saw a funeral pyre and a young woman who was about to commit sati. He sought to dissuade the widow and the family members from the sati but to no avail. He reasoned about the children who had already lost their father and would now lose their mother, who could have taken care of them, to a practice based on silly myths. This awful practice would make those children orphans.

In 1802, Lord Wellesley asked Carey to institute an inquiry into sati. Carey sent out people who investigated carefully the cases of sati within a thirty-mile radius of Calcutta and discovered 438 widow burnings in a single year. Armed with these facts, Carey implored the government to ban sati, yet Lord Wellesley had to leave India before he could take action. Carey considered this battle against a social evil as a spiritual battle against religious darkness and the forces of death. He prayed and got others to pray. One of his prominent prayer partners in this matter was William Wilberforce.

Carey's great day came when, on December 4, 1829, Lord Cavendish Bentinck, after one year of careful study, declared sati both illegal and criminal under the Bengal Code. The Edict was sent to Carey for translation two days later. Carey jumped with joy. At long last, widows were legally free to live as human beings and no longer would children be cruelly orphaned in the name of "religion."

Fifth, William Carey was able to advance the education of women. One of Carey's colleagues, Hannah Marshman took on the education problem. She started a boarding school for the children of missionaries and other Europeans. By the end of the first year in 1801, the boarding school showed a profit. With this success, Mrs. Marshman was able to start schools for the Indian boys and girls.

The success resulted in the establishment of the Calcutta Baptist Female School Society in 1819 and an additional school for girls in Calcutta. During 1820-30, Carey's mission took the lead in initiating the revolution of modern education for the women of rural Bengal. Their initiative, in turn, led to the founding of other girls' schools in Benares, Dacca and Allahabad. These schools educated children picked up from the streets and of no caste. Free schools for the low castes and the outcastes were always a chief feature of Carey's work and these were started within a twenty-mile radius of his mission, where almost 8,000 children attended.

Sixth, Carey encouraged a Scottish Missionary, Alexander Duff, to start educational institutions that imparted European Education in English language. Carey's own schools used vernacular languages as the medium or vehicle of imparting European education. Duff's efforts began to bring India into the family of English speaking nations.

Seventh, Carey focused on creating literary languages for the Indians. It was not English, but their native vernaculars, including Hindi. During India's great linguistic debate in the 1820s and 30s, Carey's work was honored by both the parties – the Classists who argued that Sanskrit, Persian, or Arabic should be taught in order to enrich the vernaculars and the Anglists, who argued in favor of English. Lord Macaulay – in many ways a protégé of William Wilberforce – who finally ruled in favor of English, did so in the spirit of William Carey. He wanted English literature to enrich Indian vernaculars.

Charles Grant's *Observations*, which was well received in Britain's political circles, argued that the commercial interests of England would be better served by improving India, not by enslaving it. That this viewpoint finally won the day was illustrated when, forty years later, in a speech in Parliament in 1833, Lord Macaulay built upon Grant's thesis. In that historic speech Macaulay argued the England must pursue this policy of improving India, even if improvement meant India's eventual independence. For, "To trade with civilized men is infinitely more profitable than to govern savages." The following is a sample of the power of Macaulay's language and logic that overwhelmed Parliament.

> It may be that the public mind of India may expand under our system till it has outgrown that system; that by good Government we may educate our subjects into a capacity for better Government, that having become interested in European knowledge, they may in some future age, demand European institutions (of freedom). Whether such a day will ever come I know not. But never will I attempt to avert or retard it. Whenever it comes it will be the proudest day in English history. To have found a great people sunk in the lowest depths of slavery and superstitions, to have so ruled them as to have made them desirous and capable of all the privileges of citizens, would indeed be a title to glory all our own. The scepter may pass away from us. Unforeseen accidents may derange our most profound schemes of policy. Victory may be inconstant to our arms. But there are triumphs which are followed by no reverse. There is an empire exempt from all natural cause of decay. Those triumphs are the pacific triumphs of reason over barbarism; that empire is the imperishable empire of our arts and our morals, our literature and our laws.

Charles Trevelyan, Macaulay's brother-in-law, summed up the long term aim of the Christian reform movement in 1838 in his pamphlet on Education in India. Macaulay and Trevelyan were articulating what Carey and Duff had already practiced and demonstrated. Trevelyan wrote:

> The existing connection between two such distant countries as England and India, cannot, in the nature of things, be permanent: No effort of policy can prevent the natives from ultimately regaining their independence. But there are two ways of arriving at this point. One of these is through the medium of revolution; the other through that of reform...(Revolution) must end in the

complete alienation of mind and separation of interests between ourselves and the natives; the other (reform) in a permanent alliance, founded on mutual benefit and good-will. The only means at our disposal for preventing (revolution) and securing...the results (of reform) is, to set the natives on a process of European improvement...The natives will have independence, after first learning how to make good use of it; and we shall exchange profitable subjects for still more profitable allies...Trained by us to happiness and independence, and endowed with our learning and political institutions. India will remain the proudest monument of British benevolence.

The long anticipated day of India's independence and the triumph of the Christian reformers ultimately came in 1947. India asked for and became independent of the British Raj. Yet it retained and resolved to live by British laws and institutions, as a member of the British Commonwealth. For example, the Indian Penal Code of 1861, which is still the basis of law in Indian jurisprudence, was drafted by Macaulay himself as "Codes of Criminal and Civil Procedures" when he served as India's law minister.

Thus, India's independence in 1947 was not only a victory for Mahatma Gandhi and the "freedom fighters," but even more fundamentally, a triumph for Carey's Christian England. It marked the victory of the early missionaries over the narrow commercial, political and military vested interests of England, as well as a victory for the hearts and minds of India.

Does the 21st Century Need Reformers?

Today, the long term results of the battles fought by Grant, Carey, Wilberforce, Macaulay, and Trevelyan are visible to everyone. Their educational, linguistic, moral, and socio-political mission was India's "Grand Experiment". Their success has become the bedrock for the limited success of the present and the unlimited promise for the future. Yet, it would be foolish to ignore Macauly's wise words that none of us can predict or control the future, for "Unforeseen accidents may derange our most profound schemes of policy." We need to follow these great men and look at the challenges of our times – the perils that can once again turn promises into quagmires. The following five challenges have the capacity to derange the calculations of our best economists:
1) The Caste Conflict
2) Hindu-Muslim Communal Conflict
3) Uncontrolled Urbanization
4) Corruption
5) HIV/AIDS

The Caste Conflict

So far, the upper castes have been the primary beneficiaries of education and democracy. However, enough has filtered down to awaken India's lower castes. They are no longer prepared to accept an inferior status. They have acquired enough strength to challenge Hindu social system and the philosophical ideas of karma, reincarnation, and dharma that sustain Hinduism. India has arrived at the point where France was before the French Revolution. Interestingly, the main safety valve that India has to escape a French Revolution is the one that William Wilberforce fought for – individual liberty to reject a religion that promotes inequality in favor of a religion that promotes equality. Political democracy is fuelling a hunger for social and spiritual democracy – for human equality and "priesthood of all believers". Brahmins have a vested interest in preserving their millennia old honor and privileges. They may even have the motivation to fight to preserve the status quo. But an all-out clash of castes could derail India.com project.

The Communal Conflict

India has become the biggest beneficiary of President Bush's war on terror. That war turned the government of Pakistan against the terrorists who used to intensify the Hindu/Muslim tensions in India. However, there are good reasons to believe that the war on terror has radicalized Pakistani Muslims. A democratic election in Pakistan is likely to throw up a radical Muslim government, which will have a vested interest in fuelling communal tensions in India. During the previous six decades the frequent Hindu-Muslim riots in India used to hurt the Muslim economy. The future rioters and terrorists are likely to target the rising economic power of the Hindus.

Urbanization or Slumification

The socialist economics made some difference to the traditional Hindu economic order, but the socialist "land-reforms" deceived so many people that at least sixty-percent of India survives on subsistence agricultural economy. The technological fact is that India does not need more than 10% of her population growing food for everyone. This means that 50% of India (500 million people) will have to move from the village to the city. That could translate into 100 cities receiving 4-5 million people each. That in turn means a slumification of our prestigious cities such as Bangalore. This projected slumification would lead to an all-round urban nightmare. It will have a bearing on caste and communal conflicts as well as on politics, corruption, and HIV/AIDs issues mentioned below. The challenge of this social chaos is that unless potential investors recover the mettle of earlier reformers, slumification would redirect the investors to more orderly cities in other countries.

Corruption

Corruption was a key factor that turned the promise of India into a great peril or quagmire for the East India Company. During the last decade the corruption of India's political class played a significant role in ruining Enron. It will hurt many more multi-national companies in the days ahead. India's multi-party democracy is enabling new and small caste based parties to acquire power. These parties may be small but they have big appetite for power and bribes. Therefore, once a company sets up a significant base in a corrupt state, it has to appease potential troublemakers. It is vulnerable to be bled to death by petty politicians. This factor implies that the mission of Grant, Carey, and Wilberforce – India's moral renewal – is as important today as it was in their day.

HIV-AIDS

Experts say that India is set to become the world capital of HIV/AIDS. This is no place to examine the implications of this fact, but it needs no imagination to understand that it would be hard for a nation to realize its potential if its workforce – the young adults – are laid off work in millions and if the state becomes responsible for millions of young orphans.

Although each of these problems requires distinct strategies and action programs, they are all intertwined and spring from deeper springs of culture and worldview. They reinforce and complicate each issue and have cumulative impact. Together they send out one message: India has always a land of promise but thanks to the new wave of "reforms" India has once again opened up to the world. However, the perils are as real today as they were in the eighteenth century. These perils call our generation to produce new heroes – men and women like Charles Grant, William Carey, and William Wilberforce.

The Theology of William Carey

Bruce J. Nicholls

Bruce J. Nicholls was a career missionary in India working in theological education and in pastoral ministry with the Church of North India, then executive secretary of the World Evangelical Fellowship (now World Evangelical Alliance) Theological Commission 1968-1988 and Editor of the Evangelical Review of Theology for 18 years and is now Editor of the Asia Bible Commentary series and seen as an outstanding elder statesman in missiology and theological education all over the world. He authored and edited dozens of books in his long career.

World Evangelical Fellowship. Theological Commission. (2000, 1993). Evangelical Review of Theology: Volume 17. "A digest of articles and book reviews selected from publications worldwide for an international readership, interpreting the Christian faith for contemporary living." (electronic ed.). Logos Library System; Evangelical Review of Theology (369). Carlisle, Cumbria, UK: Paternoster Periodicals.

Little has been written on Carey's theology. It was more implicit in his correspondence and work than explicit. Except for the Enquiry which Carey published before he left England, we have little to guide us. In this article I seek to probe five areas of Carey's theological concerns. More research is needed if we are to understand better Carey's motivation, his priorities and his message.

Editor of the ERT

William Carey's involvement in evangelism, church planting, language learning, translation work and institutional building left him no time for theological reflection. His gifts lay in linguistics and administration and not in theological formulations. No record of his sermons remains. The *Enquiry*, his letters, articles in the *Friends of India* and *Samarchar Darpan* and the numerous biographies are the only source materials for understanding and evaluating his theology. It is clear that his general theological outlook took shape during his youthful years in England prior to sailing to India in June 1793. He was caught up in the impact of the first Evangelical Awakening of the 18th Century which impacted the lives of the working class people in rural England as well as in the towns and cities. John Wesley was at the heart of this movement. Its theological origins were in the Protestant Reformation but spiritually it was in the succession of the mystical and ascetic traditions of the medieval and early Church, the Puritan revival of the 17th Century and the pietism of the Moravian movement in Germany. John Wesley's theology led him in the direction of Arminianism while Whitefield and Jonathan Edwards in the American colonies were more influenced by the Puritan Calvinism. His own particular group of dissenters, the Particular Baptists were Calvinistic while the General Baptists were more moderate. Carey was caught in this tension, as is clearly evident in the *Enquiry*.

Biblical Foundations

The Bible was the common manifesto of the Evangelical Movement and it became the controlling factor in Carey's life. His conversion experience which began under the influence of his fellow apprentice journeyman shoemaker John Warr in his 17th year, was the turning point of his life. He left the Church of England and was baptized as a believer four years later (7th October 1783). During this period Carey's theology was shaped by his close association with the leaders of the Northamptonshire Baptist churches and in particular by John Ryland, Andrew Fuller, Robert Hall Snr. and John Sutcliff. Carey became 'an ardent student of the scriptures'. From a New Testament commentary on the shelf of his employer Clarke Nichols, Carey was introduced to the Greek text. Thereafter Latin, Greek and later Hebrew, became the centre of his studies and the foundation for his later translation work. He studied the Bible with implicit trust in its truthfulness, reliability and authority all of which characterized the Evangelical Movement. For Carey the Bible was the word of God to be loved and obeyed. His passion was to be a preacher of the Word.

Carey's hermeneutical principles were literalistic and uncomplicated. He took literally the commands of Jesus and expected God to fulfil his promises. The Bible was his sole means of knowing the truth of God and the way of salvation. An example of his proof text method was his use of the Great Commission of Matthew 28:18-20 in his pioneering booklet *An Enquiry into the Obligations of Christians to use means for the Conversion of the Heathens*. David Bosch notes that Carey 'based his entire case on the argument that the Great Commission (Matthew 28:18-20) was as valid in his day (1792) as it had been in the days of the Apostle'.[91] On this basis Carey stressed the obligation of Christians to proclaim the gospel worldwide and to use every means possible for the conversion of those who heard it.

Carey followed the expository model of the Baptist preachers of Northamptonshire. This can be seen in his so-called 'Deathless Sermon'

---

[91] David J. Bosch, 'The How and Why of a True Biblical Foundation for Missions', Zending op weg Naor de Toekopmst (Kampen U.J.H. Kok. 1978), p. 34.

preached to seventeen pastors of the Northamptonshire Association of Baptist churches on the 31st May 1792. With graphic illustrations on enlarging the tent Carey expounded Isaiah 54:v2, dividing the text into his two memorable principles, 'Expect great things from God. Attempt great things for God.'[92] This sermon proved to be a milestone in Carey's appeal to Andrew Fuller and others to form the Baptist Missionary Society, an event which took place four months later. The sermon reflects Carey's confidence in the sovereignty of God and his love for the world and his own certainty of the need to use every possible means to proclaim the gospel worldwide.

Throughout Carey's forty years of missionary service in India he was motivated by this consuming passion to translate the Bible into as many languages of the common people as possible so that all might hear and believe the gospel. Like other evangelicals of his day Carey believed that unless the heathen hear the gospel they are eternally lost; a conviction that continues to motivate evangelical missionaries today.

Christology for Mission

William Carey's theology was clearly Christocentric. Jesus Christ was the centre of his spiritual pilgrimage and the only hope for the salvation of the world. Having imbibed the piety of Moravian missionaries and having been inspired by the prayer life of David Brainerd (missionary to the American Indians), Carey was disciplined in maintaining his daily early morning devotional life of Bible reading and prayer. He often talked aloud with his Lord as he walked in his garden. Carey sought to bring every thought captive to Christ and he refused to speculate beyond the revelations of scripture. It cannot be over-emphasized that the cross was the centre of his preaching whether in the church or in the bazaar. He believed Christ's death was a substitutionary atonement for sin. In preaching the cross, Carey called upon his hearers to repent of their sins and put their trust in Christ for salvation alone. He had little confidence in himself and through the stress and sorrows of his missionary career Carey turned again and again to his Lord for solace and strength. This is beautifully illustrated in the epitaph he prepared for himself, taken from the first couplet of Isaac Watt's hymn:

---

[92] A. Christopher Smith has argued that the words 'from God' and 'for God' were not part of the original sermon. See A. Christopher Smith, 'The Spirit and Letter of Carey's Catalytic Watchword' (*Baptist Quarterly* 33, January 1990, 266-37).

A guilty weak and helpless worm,
On thy kind arms I fall.
Be thou my strength and righteousness
My Jesus – and my all.

This moving testimony reveals Carey's humble piety, his Christ-centred hope and his trust in the sovereign grace of God. His sense of personal unworthiness before the righteousness of God sheds light on his Calvinistic faith. There is no doubt that his moderate Calvinism had sustained him through the crises in his life. It is also reflected in his love of nature as the handiwork of the Creator. He does not appear to have given very much emphasis to the work of the Holy Spirit as in the later Missionary Movement. Carey was a man of the Book and of his Lord, Jesus Christ.

In these early years, Carey the pastor felt deeply the conflict among his contemporaries concerning the sovereignty of God and human obligation to proclaim the gospel. The alleged comment of John Ryland Sr. at a ministerial fraternal of the Baptist Association about 1786 hurt him deeply. In response to his questioning as to whether the Lord's command was still binding, Ryland is supposed to have replied 'Young man, sit down. When God pleases to convert the heathen, he'll do it without consulting you or me. Besides, there must be another Pentecostal gift of tongues!'[93]

The Gathered Church

William Carey's theology was not only Christ-centred; it was Church-centred. Having left the Anglican Church of his fathers, Carey became an enthusiastic Dissenter and a committed member of the Particular Baptist church in which he had been baptized. Following Carey's baptism at the age of 22, John Sutcliff, the pastor at Olney, recognized his gifts and encouraged him to seek recognition as a lay preacher. This led to his being called as pastor to the village church of Moulton in 1787 and two years later to the Harvey Lane Baptist Church at Leicester. His six years in pastoral ministry, much of which was spent in controversy owing to the low level of spirituality in his churches, laid the foundation of his Church-centred understanding of mission. Here too he was influenced by his friends John Ryland, Andrew Fuller and John Sutcliff. It was to be expected that the missionary structure Carey pioneered was a denominational one.

---

[93] There is no proof that these were Ryland's exact words. His son, John Ryland Jnr. denied the authenticity of the anecdote. See Iain H. Murray, 'William Carey: Climbing the Rainbow', *The Banner of Truth*, October 1992, p. 21, n. 1.

Carey's Doctrine of the Church followed the 'primitive' New Testament model which stressed preaching, spontaneous spirituality in worship, emphasis on fellowship, the ordinances of believers' baptism and on the Lord's Supper and on independency in church organization.[94] Carey carried this model to India. It is significant that with the arrival of the new missionaries in Serampore early in the year 1800, Carey and his colleagues immediately constituted themselves as the local Baptist Church and elected Carey as pastor. The first convert, Krishna Pal, upon his baptism in December 1800, was admitted without delay to the membership of this church and invited to participate in the service of the Lord's Supper. Thus the concept of the gathered church with its emphasis on the fellowship of believers became the guiding principle of Carey's evangelistic and church planting ministries.

Carey and his colleagues carried this principle into the structuring of the Serampore Mission. As a community they covenanted together to live as an extended family, sharing in a common table, common purse and in rotating leadership. Carey had been inspired to follow this joint family lifestyle by the example of the Moravian missionaries, except in the concept of a permanent house father. In October 1805 they drew up a 'Form of Agreement' in which in eleven points they outlined their Mission strategy. This included the resolution that the church must be indigenous from the beginning. The 8th principle stated: 'it is only by means of native preachers that we can hope for the universal spread of the Gospel throughout this immense continent. We think it is our duty as soon as possible, to advise the native brethren who may be formed into separate churches, to choose their pastors and deacons from their own countrymen.'[95]

It was often stated that Carey failed as an evangelist and in establishing new churches. John Mack of Serampore College, in a funeral sermon on Carey (reprinted in the *Bengal Hurkaru*, Calcutta 14th August 1834) remarked that he had never heard of a single Indian converted directly by Carey's preaching and that in the last twelve years of his life Carey only once, to his knowledge, addressed the gospel to 'the heathen'.[96] This harsh judgement hardly does justice to the priority Carey gave to preaching and

---

[94] Christopher Smith contrasts the 'primitive' model with the 'professional' institutional model of the later church. He argues that the Serampore trio operated simultaneously in the spiritual world of personal piety and the commercial world of technologically-impressive capitalism. See his article 'A Tale of Many Models', *International Bulletin of Missionary Research 1992*.

[95] Cited *Christian History* (Vol. XI. No. 4), p. 34.

[96] E. Daniel Potts, *British Baptist Missionaries in India 1793-1837* (Cambridge CUP 1967), p. 35, n. 1.

to establishing new churches in the earlier years of his ministry. It is understandable that in his later years Carey was preoccupied with his translation work, his teaching at Fort William College and the founding and developing of Serampore College and he was overwhelmed by personal controversy. It is clear from his letters and biographers that in his early years in Serampore Carey preached regularly in the bazaar and entered into serious dialogue with Hindus and others. The statistics of the Serampore Mission suggest that by 1812 there were eleven Bengali churches and twenty native evangelists and by 1813 five hundred had been baptized. This would have included Anglo-Indians and Europeans as well as Hindus. These figures represent the work of the Mission as a whole, not just of Carey. Considering the suspicion and resentment of the European community, the fanaticism of the Brahmins, and the low moral standards of the people, the slow growth of the church is understandable. The Hindu reform movement beginning with Rammohan Roy after 1815 proved an effective half-way house for would-be converts from the upper classes. They accepted Christian ethical teaching but chose to remain within the Hindu caste community. In a letter to his son Jabez dated 26th January 1824, Carey shared his distress that the people seem 'as insensible as ever' to Christianity.[97] Even if Carey saw little direct fruit for his preaching he was instrumental in the conversion of many through his multi-faceted ministries.

The Serampore trio, Carey, Marshman and Ward, were much more committed to the principle of establishing indigenous churches than were the Calcutta and General Baptist missionaries. This created some friction between them. The Serampore trio recognized that native pastors needed to be properly trained and to become self supporting, and that the churches must be self governing. Their first step in this policy was to establish as many schools as possible giving a general education in the Bengali language and seeking to make the schools self-supporting. Joshua Marshman drew up guidelines in *Hints relative to Native Schools, together with an outline of an Institution for their Extension and Management*.[98] The success of their educational system led the Serampore missionaries to recognize the need for a higher institution to train teachers for the schools and to prepare native preachers as evangelists and pastors for the work of the churches. In the prospectus for the proposed College at Serampore they emphasized both Sanskrit, Eastern literature and European science and knowledge as being essential to the training of national church leaders. It is

---

[97] Potts, *ibid.*, p. 36.
[98] John D. W. Watts, 'Baptists and the Transformation of Culture: A Case Study from the Career of William Carey' *Review and Expositor* 89, (1992) No. 1, p. 16.

also significant that in addition to training Christians as teachers and evangelists they opened the College to youth from all parts of India 'without distinction in caste or creed'. Eleven Brahmin students enrolled in the first session.

The Serampore missionaries saw that though the church was called out of the world to be a new fellowship, it must be engaged in witness in the world; thus Serampore symbolized all that Carey and his colleagues stood for – respect for Indian language, literature and culture, the values of Western science and knowledge and a commitment to the message of the Bible and to Christian ethical lifestyle. The original vision for Serampore College continues to be maintained to the present day, both as a University College with faculties in Arts, Science and Commerce and as a Theological faculty for training men and women for the service of the Church.

William Carey's Doctrine of the Church was not only that of the local church but of the ecumenical family of Churches. In Calcutta Carey had a good working relationship with the evangelical Church of England chaplains. He met regularly with Henry Martyn for fellowship in the restructured pagoda at Serampore. Carey was a catalyst for world evangelization. In 1806 he proposed to Andrew Fuller, the Secretary of the Baptist Missionary Society, that they should summon 'a meeting of all denominations of Christians at the Cape of Good Hope somewhere about 1910 to be followed by another such conference every ten years'. Andrew Fuller turned the project down, replying, 'I consider this as one of Br'r Carey's pleasing dreams'.[99] It was not until the World Missionary Conference of Edinburgh in 1910 that Carey's vision was realized. In a real sense it may be said that Carey's vision for world evangelization also anticipated the slogan of the contempory Lausanne Movement for World Evangelism, 'calling the Whole Church to take the Whole Gospel to the Whole World'.

Faith and Culture

For William Carey the Christian faith and Indian culture were not irreconcilable. He strove to affirm Bengali culture where it did not conflict with the gospel so that converts could retain their cultural self-identity and give leadership in evangelism and to the emerging church. He resisted attempts to replace Indian culture by the so-called Christian culture of the west. Carey was motivated by his respect for the highest values in Indian culture

---

[99] Ruth Rouse 'William Carey's "Pleasing Dream"' *International Review of Missions* (1949) p. 181.

as well as by his conviction that evangelism was primarily the task of the national Christians.

This culture-affirming attitude was expressed in a number of ways. For example, Carey did not ask his first convert Krishna Pal to change his name even though he carried the name of a Hindu god. The prevailing spirit then and until recently was that converts at their baptism should take an anglicized biblical name or the western name of their missionary benefactor. Similarly in regard to dress, Carey and his colleagues encouraged new believers to retain their traditional dress and even the sacred thread of the higher castes.[100]

When the Brahmin convert Krishna Prasad disregarded and trampled on his sacred thread before his baptism, Ward kept it and later sent it to England for safe keeping. Then Ward gave Krishna Prasad money to buy another *paita* and for some years Krishna Prasad wore his thread on his preaching tours.

However, the most significant factor in Carey's approach to Indian culture was his insistence that education be in the vernacular language.[101] While other missionaries and social workers were emphasizing the use of the English language and western education, on the assumption that the Enlightenment culture of the west was superior to native language and culture, Carey insisted on Bengali as the medium of education from primary school through to university education in Serampore College. As we have seen, Carey recognized the importance of both Eastern and Western knowledge and these were taught side by side at Serampore College.

While endorsing Bengali cultural values Carey and his colleagues rejected those cultural practices that conflicted with biblical ethics and social justice. Carey opposed idolatrous practices such as the Jagannath festival in which worshippers lost their lives, but he did not attack idolatry as such in public.

---

[100] It is perhaps significant that despite his commitment to affirming national culture, Carey himself continued to wear the dress of his own English culture and of his status as a college professor. For Carey there was no single Christian culture; each was valid in its own context.

[101] In his translation work Carey not only translated the Bible into many Indian languages but, with Marshman, one third of the Hindu epic *Ramayana*, into Bengali (5 volumes) and with Ward into English (3 volumes). He also published *Itihasamala* in Bengali, an anthology of prose stories of Bengali life. It can be argued that he wanted to show the superiority of the teaching of the Bible to other scriptures, and at the same time win respect in official circles. This was no doubt true, but it does not fully explain the enormous effort put into this work in spite of the criticism of other missionaries and the Society in England.

The Theology of William Carey

Carey was a vigorous opponent of the evils of the caste system. Upon profession of faith, Krishna Pal was invited by Thomas and Carey to share a meal with the missionaries and so break caste. Only then was he baptized and admitted to the Church. At his first communion Krishna Prasad the Brahmin convert received the common communion cup from the hands and lips of Krishna Pal, the Sudra. This was no doubt an intentional breaking of caste. Carey's life-long campaign against the evils of infanticide and the burning of widows (*sati*) reflected his commitment to biblical ethics and to compassionate justice. Carey was committed to the social transformation of culture.

This raises an important question as to how far Carey's action for social change was the consequence of his theological convictions or of his instinctive response to injustices that he experienced in his early years. Carey was no systematic theologian and the answer is probably both/and rather than either/or. Carey's acceptance of and love for the Bible and his sense of obligation to obey its teaching shaped his faith and action. Frederick Downs argues that in the New Testament conflict between James and Paul on the issue of Gentile converts accepting Palestinian Jewish culture, Carey was clearly on the side of Paul, who recognized that there was no single Christian culture but that the Christian faith must be incarnate in every culture.[102] Yet there can be no doubt that Carey's own cultural background prepared him in a unique way to feel deeply about the injustices of Indian society. Throughout his life in England he lived in constant poverty, and as a dissenter was disadvantaged in education, employment and social acceptance. The spirit of the second half of the 18th Century in England was one of radicalism and revolt, reformers clamouring for freedom of the press and dissenters expressing their resentment of the Test and Cooperation Acts. The idealism of the French and American revolutions encouraged republican inclinations to overthrow the monarchy. Carey the young radical was caught up in this ferment. On one occasion Andrew Fuller his mentor chided him for not drinking to the King's health.[103]

Carey had also imbibed the social conscience of the pre-Victorian Evangelical Movement. Throughout his life he identified with the evangelical revolt against the slave trade. For example, he stopped eating sugar from the West Indies. In India, Carey constantly prayed for the emancipation of the West Indian slaves. With tears of joy he thanked God when the

---

[102] Frederick S. Downs 'Reflections on the Culture/Society Issue in Contemporary Mission', *American Baptist Quarterly* (December 1989) pp. 239-246.

[103] S. Pearce Carey, *William Carey* (London, Carey Press, 1934), p. 6.

news came in September 1833 of their intended release.[104] Carey's cultural background made it inevitable that he would be opposed to the many social injustices he faced during his missionary career.

Integral Mission

Another significant and abiding factor in Carey's theology was his commitment to what we may call integral mission – social justice and the renewal of society integrated with compassionate service, universal education, fearless evangelism and church planting. Carey and his colleagues, Joshua and Hannah Marshman and William Ward, without whom he would never have succeeded, were pioneers and catalysts for change 150 years ahead of their time. Carey's respect for the best of Indian language and literature, his compassion for the suffering and the oppressed, his ceaseless campaign for social justice won him the respect of both the British imperialistic bureaucrats and the social activists among Hindu Reformers such as Raja Rammohan Roy. He is called Mahatma Carey – the Great Spirit – by Hindu leaders in Bengal today. However, his policies were not accepted by all. His own Baptist missionary colleagues in Calcutta who separated themselves from him, were critical of his indigenous policies, his autocratic methods and his independent spirit. As a catalyst for change, he inevitably attracted criticism. It is Carey's translation work and his holistic approach to mission that have inspired the leaders of churches and of many Christian agencies in India today to call for the bicentenary celebrations of Carey's arrival in India on 11th November 1793. Irrespective of denominational allegiance, the churches want to recognize his unique contribution to the founding and development of Christian witness in North India. Christopher Smith notes that Carey was a self-educated tradesman who rose to become a linguist and orientalist, a penniless cottager who founded a grand scholarly institution, and a shoemaker who married an aristocratic lady. He was accessible to both the humble poor, to the Anglo Saxon middle class and to the ruling aristocracy. Smith adds: 'He was a catalyst extraordinary who operated during an unrepeatable and critical *kairos* in world history.'[105] He belongs to the whole Church and to India.

As we have already suggested, Carey's theology was shaped by his biblical faith, his social background and early struggles, the radical spirit of his age and by the impact of the Evangelical pre-Victorian Movement for

---

[104] Carey, *ibid.*, p. 436.
[105] A. Christopher Smith, 'The Legacy of William Carey', *International Bulletin of Missionary Research* (16/1, 1992), p. 7.

social reform. *The Enquiry* represents the summation of his thinking prior to going to India. During his forty year missionary career he built on this foundation and made no radical departure from it. His thought naturally matured and his commitment to holistic and integral mission strengthened, despite the fact that he himself became less involved in direct evangelistic work. It has been left to others to build on these foundations.

Carey's working relationship with William Ward from 1800 until Ward's sudden death in 1823 and with Joshua and Hannah Marshman until his own death in 1834 is unique in the history of missions. Although different in temperament they were of one heart and mind in their mision. Without Ward and the Marshmans, Carey would never have achieved his holistic and integral Mission.

Part of the Serampore Mission's unique contribution to missions was their ability to develop structures and institutions to carry through the functional programmes they initiated. For example, William Ward pioneered the printing press as a vehicle to publish Carey's biblical translations and as a means of self-support for the Serampore Mission. Carey and Marshman opened numerous schools to give education to the poor. Again, Carey and Marshman established Serampore College to provide training for Indian pastors and teachers for the schools. Carey started a Savings Bank to enable the poor to provide for the education of their children and to assist the unemployed. He was instrumental in the founding of the Agro-Horticulture Society in order to raise the level of agricultural production to provide a better diet for the poor. He entered into an ongoing dialogue with the political leaders to carry through the needed social reforms. He appealed directly to the British authorities in India and to the Parliament in London. In the periodicals which he and Marshman founded, *Samachar Darpan* and *Friend of India*, they brought to the attention of their political rulers cases of infanticide, *sati*, the ill treatment of lepers and instances of slavery. They believed that word and deed were inseparable. Thus by every means Carey and his colleagues sought to arouse the consciences of both the educated national leaders and their people and the political authorities on issues of social injustice. The two most notable examples of Carey's successful influence on the political structures were the action of the Governor General Lord Wellesley in 1802 to make the practice of infanticide illegal, and the action of Governor General Lord Bentinck in abolishing *sati* in December 1829. The latter action was the culmination of Carey's protest against this social evil from the beginning of his ministry in Serampore thirty years before. At the same time it is probable that Carey's efforts inspired Rammohan Roy in his campaign against *sati*. It appears that these two leaders rarely met.

The work of William Carey cannot be judged only by the immediate successes and failures of the Serampore Mission, for as his friend Christopher Anderson declared in a memorial sermon in Edinburgh in 1834, Carey's labours, however great, were 'chiefly preparatory or prospective.'[106] Carey expected great things from God and he attempted great things for God. He was a man of vision and a man of action. Some of Carey's achievements have stood the test of time, notably Serampore College; others have not. His translation of the Bible into the languages of India was less than satisfactory and has been replaced by others, especially those working under the guidance of the Bible Society. Yet his Bengali grammar and his 87,000 word *Dictionary of the Bengali Language* (1824) helped to raise Bengali from an unsettled dialect to the level of a national language. Carey's role in the Bengali Renaissance is acknowledged by all. In the words of John Watts, 'Carey embraced Bengali and Asian culture in the name of Christ and accomplished much more for the Kingdom and for humanity than he could ever know. And generations rise up to call him blessed.'[107]

Despite the limitations of Carey's work as an evangelist, his principles for indigenous self-supporting churches are standard practices today. The heart of Carey's theology is summed up in the words he whispered to Alexander Duff on his death bed: 'Mr Duff, you have been speaking about Dr Carey, Dr Carey: when I am gone say nothing about Dr Carey. Speak only about Dr Carey's Saviour.'[108]

---

[106] Smith *ibid.*, p. 7.
[107] Watts *op. cit.*, p. 19.
[108] Pearce Carey, *op. cit.*, p. 428.

Be keen to get going

By Thomas Schirrmacher

Prof. Dr. theol. Dr. phil. Thomas Schirrmacher, PhD, DD is director of the International Institute for Religious Freedom (Bonn, Cape Town, Colombo), Professor of the Sociology of Religion at the State University of the West in Timisoara (Romania) and Distinguished Professor of Global Ethics and International Development at William Carey University in Shillong (Meghalaya, India), as well as speaker for human rights of the World Evangelical Alliance, speaking for appr. 600 million Christians. He is member of the board of the International Society for Human Rights. His newest publications include books on 'Fundamentalism', 'Racism', and 'Christians and Democracy'.

Reprinted from: Be Keen to Get Going: William Careys Theology. RVB: Hamburg, 2008².

I. Carey's Theology – the 'Missing Link'

Almost nothing about Carey's theology

William Carey is considered the "Father of Protestant missions"[109]. His book, "An Enquiry into the Obligations of Christians to Use Means for the Conversion of the Heathens"[110], written in 1792, was the beginning of the so-called 'Great Century'[111] (1792-1914) between the French and the Russian Revolutions. For the centennial anniversary, none lesser than the mentor of German missiology, Gustav Warneck, wrote, "Thus, the year 1792

---

[109] Ralph D. Winter, Steven C. Hawthorne, ed., *Perspectives on the World Christian Movement* (Pasadena: William Carey Library, 1981), p. 227-228. E. Daniels Potts, *British Baptist Missionaries in India 1793-1837: The History of Serampore and its Missions* (Cambridge: At the University Press, 1967), p. 5, criticizes this view.

[110] Edition used: William Carey, *An Enquiry into the Obligations of Christians to Use Means for the Conversion of the Heathens* (London: The Carey Kingsgate Press, 1961).

[111] Charles L. Chaney, *The Birth of Missions in America* (South Pasadena: William Carey Library, 1976), p. xi.

may be considered the true birth date of modern missions."[112] Less than twenty days after the publication of the "Enquiry", Carey preached his sermon on Isaiah 54:2-3 and began to disseminate it with a clear appeal for missions to his fellow pastors,[113] which soon led to the foundation of the mission society "The Particular Baptist Mission". The first mission society without state supervision was founded on different lines than the Anglo-Saxon honor societies.[114]

Much has been written about Carey and his colleagues, their mission field in Serampore, as well as their achievements in printing, Bible translation, teaching and in many other areas.

Strangely enough, however, in his numerous[115] biographies[116] little attention has been paid to his theology, as expressed in his major work, not

---

[112] Gustav Warneck, "Zum Jubiläumsjahr der evangelischen Mission", *Allgemeine Missions-Zeitschrift* 19 (1892) pp. 3-4. Warneck mentions Carey's predecessors, but considers their efforts private attempts, while Carey initiated the systematic spread of the Evangelical faith. In Serampore, Carey and his team took over the work of the Herrnhuter missionaries, Schmidt and Grassmann, who had begun their work in 1777. Schmidt died twelve years later, the station was closed in 1787, and Grassmann returned to Europe in 1792; from A. Schillbach, "William Carey: Eine Jubiläumserinnerung", *Zeitschrift für Missionskunde und Religionswissenschaft* 7 (1892) pp. 175-183, 219-227, and 8 (1893) pp. 29-38. For a thorough comparison of the two positions, see Aalbertinus Hermen Oussoren, *William Carey, Especially his Missionary Principles* (Diss.: Freie Universität Amsterdam), (Leiden: A. W. Sijthoff, 1945), pp. 219-269.

[113] Mary Drewery, *William Carey* (Grand Rapids: Zondervan, 1979) p. 39. James R. Beck, *Dorothy Cary: A Biography* (Grand Rapids: Zondervan, 1979) p. 65-66. Gustav Warneck, "Zum Jubiläumsjahr der evangelischen Mission", op. cit., p. 3.

[114] R. Pierce Beaver, *All Love Excelling: American Protestant Women in World Mission* (Grand Rapids: Wm. B. Eerdmans, 1968) p. 15-17.

[115] See Ernest A. Payne, "Carey and his Biographers," *The Baptist Quarterly* 19 (1961) p. 4-12, for a survey of older biographies.

[116] Works with notes and documentation: Mary Drewery, *William Carey*, op. cit.; James R. Beck, op. cit.; Works without documentation: Frank Deauville Walker, *William Carey* (1925, repr. Chicago: Moody Press, 1980); Kellsye Finnie, *William Carey*, (Carlisle, G. B.: OM Publ, and Didcot., G. B.: Baptist Missionary Society, 1992); Basil Miller, *William Carey: The Father of Modern Missions*, (Minneapolis: Bethany House, n. d.), Original title published as *William Carey: Cobbler to Missionary*, (Grand Rapids: Zondervan, 1952); S. Pearce Carey, *William Carey*, original from 1923/1934 ed. by Peter Masters (London: The Wakeman Trust, 1993), German ed.: S. Pearce Carey, *William Carey: Der Vater der modernen Mission*, (Bielefeld: CLV, 1998). See also more the specific, documented studies by A. Christopher Smith, "William Carey", *Mission Legacies: Biographical Studies of Leaders of the Modern Missionary Movement*, ed. Gerald H. Anderson American Society of Missiology Series 19 (Maryknoll, N. Y.: Orbis Books, 1994)

even in Bruce J. Nichols' article "The Theology of William Carey"[117]. (The only exception I know of is Iain Murray's study, *The Puritan Hope*).[118] This failure, probably, is due to the fact that Carey's theology differs from that of presently predominant, Post-Classical mission societies, which happily claim him as their father, although he was a Calvinist and a Postmillennialist.[119] Even the two dissertations discussing his achievements[120] ignore large areas of his theology. Neither mention his eschatological views, which played a major role in his decisions. The best description –actually a biography of his first wife[121] – mentions his personal optimism in the chapter on "Attitudes Towards the Future",[122] but not

---

[reprint of A. Christopher Smith, "The Legacy of William Carey", *International Bulletin of Missionary Research* 16 (1992) pp. 2-8]; A. Christopher Smith, "Myth and Missiology: A Methodological Approach to Pre-Victorian Mission of the Serampore Trio", *International Review of Mission* 83 (1994) pp. 451-475; and A. Christopher Smith, "The Edinburgh Connection: Between the Serampore Mission and Western Missiology", *Missiology: An International Review* 18 (1990) pp. 185-209.

[117] Bruce J. Nichols. "The Theology of William Carey". pp. 114-126, J. T. K. Daniel, Roder E. Hedlund ed., *Carey's Obligation and Indian Renaissance* (Serampore, India: Council of Serampore College, 1993)

[118] Iain Murray, *The Puritan Hope: Revival and the Interpretation of Prophecy* (Edinburgh: Banner of Truth Trust, 1971) pp. 138-147. One should also mention Brian Stanley, *The History of the Baptist Missionary Society 1792-1992* (Edinburgh: T & T. Clark, 1992) pp. 36-57, even though Stanley is dealing with the views of all members of the Serampore-Trio. Stanleys view is, that the work in Serampore rested especially on belief in the sovereignty of God and on the plan to plant indigenous churches under indigenous leadership.

[119] J. A. de Jong, *As the Waters Cover the Sea: Millennial Expectations in the Rise of Anglo-American Missions 1640-1810* (Kampen: J. H. Kok:, 1970) p. 176-181. W. Bieder, "William Carey 1761-1834", *Evangelisches Missions-Magazin* 105 (1961) pp. 153-173, here pp. 172-173. Bieder holds Carey for an example for all "Reformed Christians" (p. 172).

[120] Aalbertinus Hermen Oussoren, *William Carey, Especially his Missionary Principles*, op. cit., includes an excellent historical discussion of his life pp. 19-121.; E. Daniels Potts. *British Baptist Missionaries in India 1793-1837: The History of Serampore and its Missions*, (Cambridge: University Press, 1967), contains the most thorough work on Carey and the work of his team in India.

[121] James R. Beck, op. cit. This work rises above the usual prejudices against Carey's marriage to an uneducated woman, for which one might find the following example: W. Bieder, "William Carey 1761-1834", op. cit., pp. 153-173. After the death of his first wife, Carey was happily married for 13 years (1807-1821) with the linguistically gifted Danin Charlotte Rumohr. His third wife, Grace Hughes, survived him. Both these marriages are little known. See also A. Christopher Smith, "William Carey", op. cit., p. 248.

[122] James R. Beck, op. cit., p. 130.

his optimistic perspective on world missions, which he derived from his Postmillennial theology.

German[123] speaking theologians have shown little interest[124] in Carey's "Enquiry" although Protestant mission societies continually refer to his work as the origin of their own.[125] The German edition, which identified the geographical details for the first time,[126] did not appear until 1993.[127] In 1987, the first German biography of Carey was published.[128] A work,

---

[123] Here I would like to recommend the Swedish articles in SMT: "Arvet efter William Carey"; *Svensk Missionstidskrift* 80 (1/1992) p. 6-23. They include a Swedish translation of the "Enquiry" (without the graphs) as well as the following articles; Göran Janzon, "Introduktion: William Carey och Hans Berömda 'Undersökning'", p. 1-5; Torsten Bergsten, "William Carey och Serampore-Missionen", p. 24-38; Ulla Sandgren, "William Carey och Bibeln Till Indiens Folk", p. 39-46. None of these pieces, however, deal with Carey's eschatology.

[124] E. Wallroth, "William Carey", *Allgemeine Missions-Zeitschrift* 14 (1887) pp. 97-123; Johann Schmidt, "Carlotte Emilia von Rumohr und William Carey: Ein früher Beitrag Schleswig-Holsteins zur Mission in Indien", *Schriften des Vereins für Schleswig-Holsteinische Kirchengeschichte* II, Reihe Beiträge und Mitteilungen 28, (1972), pp. 38-51: W. Bieder, "William Carey 1761-1834", op. cit., which on page 154, Note 1, lists older texts in the Baseler Missionsbibliothek on Carey. Most are inspirational texts, predominantly in German. Some of the best inspirational biographies in German are G. Schott, *William Carey, der Vater der gegenwärtigen Missionsbewegung*, Missionsschriften 164 (Barmen: Verlag des Rheinischen Missionshauses, 1915) (English original unknown) and B. Schmidt, *William Carey, der Missionspionier in Indien* (Kassel: J. G. Oncken, 1922).

[125] Particularly on the occasion of the centennial of his major work. See: A. Schillbach, op. cit., and A. Schillbach, "William Carey als Bahnbrecher der evangelischen Mission", *Evangelisches Missions Magazin* (1892) pp. 129-141, 177-186, 240-250 (p. 130 on the importance of the jubilee). This last includes a good bibliography. See also Gustav Warneck, "Zum Jubiläumsjahr der evangelischen Mission", op. cit.

[126] In the German text and in an English appendix.

[127] William Carey, *Eine Untersuchung über die Verpflichtung der Christen, Mittel einzusetzen für die Bekehrung der Heiden*, edition afem – mission classics 1, ed. and translated by Klaus Fiedler and Thomas Schirrmacher (Bonn: Verlag für Kultur und Wissenschaft, 1993). The first excerpt of the "Enquiry" in German appeared in Werner Raupp, *Mission in Quellentexten: Geschichte der Deutschen Evangelischen Mission von der Reformation bis zur Weltmissionskonferenz 1910* (Bad Liebenzell, Germany: Verlag der Liebenzeller Mission; und Erlangen, Germany: Verlag der Evangelisch-Lutherischen Mission, 1990) p. 231-235. (Good bibliography on page 235).

[128] Harald Schilling, "Der geistige und geistliche Werdegang William Careys bis zu seiner Veröffentlichung der Enquiry im Jahr 1782", *Fundierte Theologische Abhandlungen Nr. 5* (Wuppertal, Germany: Verlag der Evangelischen Gesellschaft für Deutschland, 1987) pp. 77-92.

which, however, only described his life up to the publication of the "Enquiry" and has little to say about his theology.

This fact is even more surprising, for Carey was not a pioneer missionary who, due to conditions, left no material for posterity. A. Christopher Smith writes, "He was much more of a mission motivator and Bible translator than a pioneer in the heart of India – or a mission strategist."[129]

The significance of Carey's work lies not in the 420 converts[130] in Serampore. As a settled and thorough designer, Carey left many texts describing his thought and his theology.[131]

Smith attempts to liberate Carey from false renown by referring to the achievements of his colleagues, William Ward and Joshua Marshman,[132] but goes too far; in my opinion. Carey's work not only consisted of the main ideas behind the "Enquiry" and the 'Baptist Mission' but also most of the task of translation. Besides, Carey's team, particularly the 'Serampore trio', Carey, Marshman and Ward, have always been properly esteemed, especially after the publication of John Clark Marshman's *The Life and Times of Carey, Marshman and Ward* in 1859.[133] "Carey was a man of team-work,"[134] writes W. Bieder, who advises the modern missionary:

> "He can learn from Carey, that it is quite possible to work for twenty three years under difficult conditions – together rather than against each other."[135]

Even E. Daniel Potts, who has best analyzed and honored the significance of the teamwork in Serampore, emphasizes Carey as the driving force behind the work.[136]

---

[129] A. Christopher Smith, "William Carey", op. cit., p. 249.
[130] According to A. Schillbach, "William Carey als Bahnbrecher der evangelischen Mission", op. cit., p. 245, for the time until 1818.
[131] John Clark Marshman, *The Life and Times of Carey, Marshman and Ward, Embracing the History of the Serampore Mission* (London: Longman, 1859). (Volume 1 up to 1812, Volume 2 1813 to Marshman's death in 1837). See also John Clark Marshman, ed., *William Carey, Letters, Official and Private* (London: 1828).
[132] A. Christopher Smith, "William Carey", op. cit., p. 246.
[133] John Clark Marshman, *The Life and Times of William Carey*, op. cit.
[134] W. Bieder. "William Carey 1761-1834", op. cit., p. 165.
[135] Ibid., p. 172.
[136] E. Daniels Potts, *British Baptist Missionaries in India 1793-1837*, op. cit., pp. 20-21.

2.1 Postmillennialism and Missions

Classical and Post-Classical Missions and Eschatology

Klaus Fiedler has suggested a good classification of Protestant mission societies.[137] "Classical" mission societies are denominational organizations that usually originate from the Reformed tradition. They began with Carey's 'Baptist Mission Society' in 1792. "Post-Classical" missions are those of the Brethren, including the so-called free missionaries, the faith missions, which, Fiedler believes, originated with Hudson Taylor (and include most modern Evangelical mission boards), and Pentecostal mission societies (movements listed in chronological order of origin). Classical mission societies arose during the first and second Great Revivals (Pietism), the Post-Classical faith missions during the third Revival (the so-called Sanctification movement).

The difference between modern 'evangelical' missions and modern 'ecumenical' missions is a century old. 'Ecumenical' missions are Classical, Reformed missions which have become liberal. Faith missions are those that differ from the Reformed theology of the Classical mission societies on various points and with varying intensity.

Eschatology is a clear example. The Classical churches tend to be A- or Postmillennial, while the Post-Classical mission boards are generally Dispensationalist or Premillennial.

Eschatology, Missions and Postmillennialism

Already in the beginning of this century, Theodor Oehler, director of the Basler Mission, observed, just as Gustav Warneck had done:

---

[137] Klaus Fiedler, *Ganz auf Vertrauen: Geschichte und Kirchenverständnis der Glaubensmissionen* TVG (Gießen, Germany: Brunnen, 1992) pp. 12-53; Klaus Fiedler, "Der deutsche Beitrag zu den interdenominationellen Missionen", in *Bilanz und Plan: Mission an der Schwelle zum Dritten Jahrtausend Festschrift George W. Peters*, Evangelische Missionslehre, Vol. C2, ed. Hans Kasdorf and Klaus W. Müller (Bad Liebenzell, Germany: VLM, 1988). See also Thomas Schirrmacher, "Hans Kasdorf/Klaus W. Müller (Hg.) Bilanz und Plan ..." *Jahrbuch Mission* 21 (1989) pp. 190-192; Klaus Fiedler, "125 Glaubensmissionen: Die Anfänge", *Evangelikale Missiologie* 5 (1989) 2, pp. 19-25; Klaus Fiedler, "Die Bedeutung der Einzigartigkeit Jesu Christi für die Theologie der Glaubensmissionen" in *Die Einzigartigkeit Jesu Christi*, ed. Rolf Hille and Eberhard Troeger (Wuppertal, Germany: Brockhaus, 1993).

"... there is an undeniable connection between missions and the Christian hope for the future: 'We will soon discover that missionary attitudes will be suppressed by a certain view of the future, which will dampen earnest motivation for missionary activity'."[138]

"Expectations on the future of God's Kingdom have not always moved in the same direction as missions, which have not served to vitalize them."[139]

Out of three most common eschatologies, Pre-, A- and Postmillennialism,[140] the latter has more often been the champion of increasing missionary fervor.

R. G. Clouse defines the role of Postmillennialism fittingly:

"In contrast to premillennialists, postmillennialists emphasize the present aspects of God's kingdom which will reach fruition in the future. They believe that the millennium will come through Christian preaching and teaching. Such activity will result in a more godly, peaceful, and prosperous world. The new age will not be essentially different from the present, and it will come about as more people are converted to Christ."[141]

One of the best-known Reformed[142] Postmillennialists, Loraine Boettner, defines Postmillennialism in his standard work, *The Millennium*,[143] as following:

---

[138] Theodor Oehler, *Die Mission und die Zukunft des Reiches Gottes*, Basler Missions-Studien (Basel: Verlag der Missionsbuchhandlung, 1902) p. 40.

[139] Ibid., p. 1. He mentions Luther and Johann Tobias Beck as examples. See below.

[140] See Thomas Schirrmacher, *Der Römerbrief* Vol. 2 (Neuhausen, Germany: Hänssler Verlag, 1994) pp. 161-191; and Thomas Schirrmacher, *Er wird regieren (Off 11,15); Gegenüberstellung von sechs Endzeitmodellen*, (Set of 8 cassette tapes with graph, Bonn: Verlag für Kultur und Wissenschaft, 1994) for a survey of the 6 major eschatological views.

[141] R. G. Clouse, "Millennium, Views of the", *Evangelical Dictionary of Theology*, ed. Walter A. Elwell (Grand Rapids: Baker Book House, 1984) p. 715.

[142] Loraine Boettner, *The Reformed Doctrine of Predestination* (1932, repr. Grand Rapids: Baker Book House, 1987); Loraine Boettner, *The Reformed Faith* (Phillipsburg, N. J.: Presbyterian § Reformed, 1983).

[143] Loraine Boettner, *The Millennium* (1957, repr. Phillipsburg, N. J.: Presbyterian § Reformed, 1984). Compare Loraine Boettner. "Die Sicht des Postmillennialismus". in: Robert G. Clouse ed., *Das Tausendjährige Reich: 4 Beiträge aus evangelikaler Sicht*, (Marburg: Edition C. Verlag der Francke-Buchhandlung, 1983) pp. 95-115 (and 39-46, 79-86, 159-166) [engl. original: Loraine Boettner, "The View of Postmillennialism", *The Meaning of the Millennium*, ed. Robert Clouse (Downers Grove, Ill.: Inter-Varsity Press, 1977)].

"Postmillennialists believe that the Kingdom of God will be realized in the present age by the preaching of the Gospel and by the saving influence of the Holy Spirit in the hearts of individuals, and that at an unknown time in the future, the whole world will be Christianized. They also believe that Christ will return at the end of the so-called Millennium, an epoch of unknown length, marked by justice and peace ... The Millennium, according to the Postmillennialist view, is a Golden Age at the end of the present dispensation, the Age of the Church."[144]

Boettner does not believe that, "there will ever be a time on earth in which all living men will be converted or when all sin will be eliminated."[145]

However, evil will be reduced to a minimum, and Christian principles will no longer be the exception, but the rule.[146] Boettner sees this achievement as the fulfillment of the Great Commission.[147]

Postmillennialism and Missions

Theologians generally ignore the origins of modern evangelical world missions in the middle of the sixteenth century. Calvinist, mostly Puritan pastors, who had immigrated to America from England, preached the Gospel to the Indians.[148] Postmillennialism was the mother of Anglo-Saxon missions, as many dissertations[149] and other studies[150] have shown.[151] This is

---

[144] Loraine Boettner, "Die Sicht des Postmillennialismus", op. cit., p. 95 (retranslated from the German); similar Loraine Boettner, *The Millennium*, op. cit., pp. 4 and 14.

[145] Loraine Boettner, "Die Sicht des Postmillennialismus", op. cit., p. 95 (retranslated from the German).

[146] Ibid.

[147] Ibid., pp. 96, 160-161.

[148] R. Pierce Beaver ed., *Pioneers in Missions: ... A Source Book on the Rise of the Amerian Missions to the Heathen* (Grand Rapids: Wm. B. Eerdmans, 1966) pp. 11-15.

[149] J. A. de Jong, *As the Waters Cover the Sea*, op. cit.; Charles L. Chaney, op. cit.; Peter Kawerau, *Amerika und die orientalischen Kirchen: Ursprung und Anfang der amerikanischen Mission und den Nationalkirchen Westasiens*, Arbeiten zur Kirchengeschichte Vol 31 (Berlin: Walter de Gruyter, 1958): Johannes van den Berg, *Constrained by Jesus Love: An Inquiry into the Motives of the Missionary Awakening in Great Britain in the Period between 1698 and 1815* (Kampen: J. H. Kok, 1956); Sidney H. Rooy, *The Theology of Missions in the Puritan Tradition: A Study of Representative Puritans: Richard Sibbes, Richard Baxter, John Eliot, Cotton Mather, and Jonathan Edwards* (Delft, Netherlands: W. D. Meinema, 1965). On Postmillennialism, see particularly the sections on Richard Sibbes, pp. 56-58 and 325-326.

true for Calvinists (Anglicans, Presbyterians and Congregationalists) as well as for Calvinist Baptists such as William Carey.

> "The eighteenth century was the great age of Postmillennialism, which played a major role in the development of missionary thought."[152]
>
> "The Postmillennialism of the eighteenth century played an important role in the development of Anglo-America missions. In the light of chiliastic expectations, British and American revival movements were considered the first signs of a great wave soon to engulf the whole world. Not only Edwards, but also English (Isaac Watts, Philipp Doddridge) and Scottish (John Willison, John Erskine) theologians related Postmillennial eschatology with revival and with the missionary idea – a combination which gave rise to the growth of organized missionary activity at the end of the century. Carey, for example, was strongly influenced by the Postmillennial view of a universal Kingdom of God."[153]

The close relationship between Postmillennialism and missions goes back past the Reformed Puritans of America and England to the Reformation.[154]

---

[150] The standard work is Iain Murray, *The Puritan Hope*, op, cit. See also, Norman Pettit, "Editor's Introduction", pp. 1-83 in Jonathan Edwards, *The Life of David Brainerd* (New Haven/London: Yale University Press, 1985) pp. 24-70; R. Pierce Beaver, "Missionary Motivation Before the Revolution", *Church History* 31 (1962) pp. 216-226 (including bibliography): R. Pierce Beaver, ed., *Pioneers in Missions*, op. cit.; Peter Toon, ed., *Puritans, the Millennium and the Future of Israel: Puritan Eschatology 1600 to 1660* (Cambridge: James Clarke, 1970).

[151] Charles Chaney, *The Birth of Missions in America*, op. cit, summarizes, "The roots of mission is in the eschatological orientation of the settlement of New England …", p. ix.

[152] Richard J. Bauckham, "Millennium", *New Dictionary of Theology*, ed. Sinclair B. Ferguson, David F. Wright and James I. Packer (Leicester, G. B. and Downers Grove, Ill.: Inter-Varsiy Press, 1989) p. 429 (retranslated from the German).

[153] Richard J. Bauckham, "Chiliasmus IV. Reformation und Neuzeit", *Theologische Realenzyklopädie*, Vol. 7, ed. Gerhard Krause and Gerhard Müller (Berlin: Walter de Gruyter, 1981) p. 741.

[154] Allen Carden, *Puritan Christianity in America* (Grand Rapids: Baker Book House, 1990) p. 94-95, 108-110: Andrew C. Rolls, "Missionary Expansion", *Encyclopedia of the Reformed Faith*, ed. Donald K. McKim (Louisville, Ky: Westminster/John Knox Press and Edinburg: Saint Andrew Press, 1992), pp. 242-244; Ernst Staehelin, *Die Verkündigung des Reiches Gottes in der Kirche Jesu Christi: Zeugnisse aus allen Jahrhunderten und Konfessionen*, Vol.5, *Von der Mitte des 17. bis zur Mitte des 18. Jahrhunderts* (Basel: Friedrich Reinhardt, 1959) pp. 5-7 on the Savoy Declaration, pp. 11-17 on John Archer and Thomas Goodwin, pp. 114-146 on John Cotten, John Eliot and Michael Wiggelsworth, p. 211-223 on Spener.

Greg L. Bahnsen mentions the Reformed[155] Postmillennialists, John Calvin,[156] Ulrich Zwingli, Theodor Bibliander of Zürich, Martin Bucer, Peter Martyr and Theodor Beza[157]; the Puritans John Cotten, Samuel Rutherford[158], John Owen[159], and Matthew Henry[160], the missionaries John Elliot[161], as well as many other missionaries of the eighteenth and nineteenth centuries[162].

Steve Schlissel has pointed out that, in the past as well as in the present, the Reformed Postmillennialists have believed in the future conversion of the Jews,[163] basing this idea primarily on Romans 11.[164] Murray considers

---

[155] On the history of Reformed Postmillennialism, see Greg Bahnsen, "The Prima Facie Acceptability of Postmillennialism", *The Journal of Christian Reconstruction* 3 no 2, (Winter 1976/77): *Symposium on the Millenium*, pp. 48-105, here pp. 68-104; Iain Murray, *The Puritan Hope*, op. cit.; Gary DeMar, Peter J. Leithart, *The Reduction of Christianity: Dave Hunt's Theology of Cultural Surrender*, (Ft. Worth, Tex.: Dominion Press & Atlanta, Georg.: American Vision Press, 1988) pp. 229-270; Joseph R. Balyeat, *Babylon: The Great City of Revelation* (Sevierville, Mich.: Onward Press, 1991). pp. 9, 42-43; Gary North ed., *Journal of Christian Reconstruction* 6 (1979) 1 (Summer), *Symposium on Puritanism and Progress*.

[156] Greg L. Bahnsen, "The Prima Facie Acceptability of Postmillennialism", op. cit., pp. 69-76; cf. the same view on Calvin's eschatology in Iain Murray, *The Puritan Hope*, op. cit., p. 40; Gary North, *Westminster's Confession: The Abandonment of Van Til's Legacy* (Tyler, Texas: Institute for Christian Economics, 1991) pp. 349-356; James Jordan, appendix, "Calvin's Millennial Confession", in John Calvin, *The Covenant Enforced, Sermons on Deuteronomy 27 and 28*, ed. James Jordan (Tyler, Texas: Institute for Christian Economics, 1990), pp. xxvi-xxxvii; Heinrich Quistorp, *Die letzten Dinge im Zeugnis Calvin's: Calvin's Eschatologie* (Gütersloh, Germany: C. Bertelsmann, 1941) p. 113-117.

[157] Greg L. Bansen, "The Prima Facie Acceptability of Postmillennialism", op. cit., p. 76.

[158] Ibid., pp. 78-79.
[159] Ibid., pp. 84-85.
[160] Ibid., pp. 88.
[161] Ibid., pp. 83-84.
[162] Ibid., pp. 94 and more.
[163] Steve M. Schlissel, "The Reformed Faith and the Jews" in *Hal Lindsey and the Reformation of the Jews*, ed. Steve. M. Schlissel and David Brown (St. Edmunton; Canada: Still Waters Revival Books, 1990) pp.17-61; Werner Keller, *Und wurden zerstreut unter alle Völker: Die nachbiblische Geschichte des jüdischen Volkes* (1966, repr. Wuppertal, Germany: R. Brockhaus, 1993) p. 490, discusses the attitude of the American Puritans. Hebrew, along with Greek and Latin, was one of the basic languages taught at Harvard College (later Harvard University) in 1636.

[164] Steve M. Schlissel, "The Reformed Faith and the Jews", op. cit., pp. 53-58. Iain Murray, *The Puritan Hope*, op. cit., has the most detailed documentation on Reformed and Puritan theologians who believed in the future conversion of Israel. He

Thomas Brightman (1562-1607) as one of the first Puritans who saw the conversion of Israel, not as the end of the world,[165] but as the beginning of the Millennium. R. J. Bauckham regards Brightman to be the "first influential exponent" of Postmillennialism.[166]

Postmillennialism is, therefore, primarily a Reformed interest. Hans Schwarz writes:

> "The Reformed tradition has often demonstrated greater closeness and support of the Postmillennial view than of other interpretations of history. To the most part, this is due to the Reformed emphasis on God's sovereignty and on the faith that Christ is Lord over all human life. They are also convinced that the Holy Spirit empowers the Christian fellowship to achieve the thorough dissemination of the world with the Gospel and the change of culture and society according to the Spirit and the will of Christ."[167]

For him, as well as for Gary DeMar,[168] Postmillennialism is an optimistic variation on Amillennialism.[169] E. L. Hebdon Taylor writes, "The Reformed faith of the Bible is future oriented."[170] Richard Bauckham, apparently an opponent of Chiliasm, still assumes that Postmillennialism was more suited to the Reformation.[171]

Therefore, it is not surprising, that Postmillennialism has been taught only in Reformed Confessions. Early Postmillennial overtones can be heard in Calvin's notes on the second petition of the Lord's Prayer in his Catechism of Geneva:

> "268. What do you understand under the 'Kingdom of God' in the second petition? It consists basically of two things: the leadership of His own through His Spirit and, in contrast to that, in the confusion and the destruction of the lost, who refuse to submit to His rule. In the end, it will be clear, that there is no power which can resist His power.

---

includes Peter Marty, Martin Bucer, Theodor Beza and the writers of the Geneva Bible. (Ibid., p. 41).

[165] Iain Murray, *The Puritan Hope*, op. cit., p. 45
[166] Richard J. Bauckham, "Millennium," op. cit., p. 429.
[167] Hans Schwarz, *Jenseits von Utopie und Resignation: Einführung in die christliche Eschatologie* (Wuppertal, Germany: R. Brockhaus, 1991), p. 205.
[168] Gary DeMar and Peter J. Leithart, *The Reduction of Christianity: Dave Hunt's Theology of Cultural Surrender* (Fort Worth, Texas: Dominion Press, and Atlanta: American Vision Press, 1988), p. 41.
[169] Hans Schwarz, *Jenseits von Utopie und Resignation*, op. cit., p. 206.
[170] E. L. Hebdon Taylor, *Economics, Money and Banking* (Nutley, N. J.: The Craige Press, 1978), p. 151.
[171] Richard J. Bauckham, "Chiliasmus IV. Reformation und Neuzeit", op. cit., p. 739.

> 269. How do you pray for the coming of this Kingdom? May the Lord increase the number of His believers from day to day, may he daily pour His gifts of grace upon them, until He has filled them completely; may He let His truth burn more brightly, may He reveal His justice, which shall confuse Satan and the darkness of His kingdom and obliterate and destroy all unrighteousness.
> 270. Does this not happen today already? Yes, in part. But we wish that it might continually grow and progress until it reaches completion on the Day of Judgment, on which God alone will rule in the high places and all creatures will bow before His greatness; He will be all in all. (1 Cor. 15:28)"[172]

Charles L. Chaney sees Calvin's view of the progress of the Kingdom of God[173] in his eschatology[174] and belief in the personal responsibility of the individual Christian towards God's Word[175], the roots of the Calvinists' later missionary fervor.

The Great Catechism of Westminster expresses a similar view in the notes of the second petition of the Lord's Prayer:

> "What do we pray for in the second petition? Answer: In the second petition (which is, Thy kingdom come), acknowledging ourselves and all mankind to be by nature under the dominion of sin and Satan, we pray, that the kingdom of Satan may be destroyed, the gospel propagated throughout the world, the Jews called, the fullness of the Gentiles brought in; the church furnished with all gospel officers and ordinances, purged from corruption, countenanced and maintained by the civil magistrate: that the ordinances of Christ may be purely dispensed, and made effectual to the converting of those that are yet in their sin, and the conforming, comforting and building up of those that already converted; that Christ would rule in our hearts here, and hasten the time of His second coming, and our reigning with Him forever and that He would be pleased so to exercise the kingdom of His power in all the world, as may best conduce to these ends."[176]

---

[172] Paul Jacobs, ed., *Reformierte Bekenntnisschriften und Kirchenordnungen in deutscher Übersetzung* (Neukirchen, Germany: Buchhandlung des Erziehungsvereins, 1949), p. 49.

[173] Charles L. Chaney, "The Missionary Dynamic in the Theology of John Calvin," *Reformed Review* 17 (Holland: 1964), pp. 24-38.

[174] Ibid., p. 34-37.

[175] Ibid., p. 29-33.

[176] James E. Bordwine, *A Guide to The Westminster Standards: Confession of Faith and Larger Catechism* (Jefferson, Md: The Trinity Foundation, 1991), p. 353-354.

The Savoy Declaration of 1658, Article 26.5, also adopted by the American Congregationalists in 1680 and 1708, adds a note which expresses Postmillennial views more clearly:[177]

> "As the LORD in care and love for his Church, hath in his infinite wise providence exercised it with great variety in all ages, for the good of them that love him, and his own glory; so according to his promise, we expect that in the latter days, Antichrist will be destroyed, the Jews called, the adversaries of the kingdom of his dear Son broken, the churches of Christ being enlarged and edified through a free and plentiful communication of light and grace shall enjoy in this world a more quiet, peaceable, and glorious condition than they have enjoyed."[178]

C. C. Geon considers this as the "first creedal statement by any confessional group to embody definite millennial presuppositions."[179]

Iain Murray

Iain Murray has further demonstrated that the notable missionaries and mission leaders, Alexander Duff,[180] David Livingstone[181], Henry Martyn[182] and Henry Venn[183], were Calvinists and Postmillennialists. Murray notes that Postmillennial expectations can be heard in the addresses accompanying the founding of the London Missionary Society in 1795, the New York Missionary Society 1797 and the Glasgow Missionary Society in 1802. The same view influenced the Church Missionary Society in 1799.[184] The London Missionary Society, an Anglican equivalent of Carey's Baptist mission, expresses Calvinistic Postmillennialism in all its documents.[185]

---

[177] See Ernst Staehelin, *Die Verkündigung des Reiches Gottes in der Kirche Jesu Christi*, op. cit., p. 5-7. See also Iain Murray, *The Puritan Hope*, op. cit., p. 53.

[178] Philipp Schaff, David S. Schaff, *The Creeds of Christendom: With a History and Critical Notes*, Vol. 3 *The Evangelical Protestant Creeds* (1931, repr. Grand Rapids, Md: Baker Book House, 1990), p. 723.

[179] C. C. Goen, "Jonathan Edwards: A New Departure in Eschatology", *Church History* 28 (1959) pp. 25-40.

[180] Iain Murray, *The Puritan Hope*, op. cit., pp. 165-171, 174-175 (Soteriology). p. 181 (Eschatology).

[181] Ibid., pp. 172-174 (Soteriology). pp. 181-183 (Eschatology).

[182] Ibid., pp. 153-154.

[183] Ibid., p. 153.

[184] Ibid., pp. 153.

[185] Ibid., pp. 146-149.

Charles L. Chaney, in a study of the early American Protestant mission boards, writes, "Not a single sermon or mission report can be discovered that does not stress eschatological considerations."[186]

---

[186] Charles L. Chaney, *The Birth of Missions in America*, op. cit., p. 269.

The early Protestant Mission Boards
All were Calvinist (Puritan, Anglican-Evangelical or Particular Baptist)
1649   The New England Company (Society for the Propagation of the Gospel in New England)
as of 1732 Supported by Society in Scotland for Propagating Christian Knowledge (founded 1701)
1762   Society for Propagating Christian Knowledge among the Indians in North America (did not last)
1787   Society for the Propagation of the Gospel among Indians and Others in North America
1787   Society for the Propagation of the Gospel among the Heathen
1792   (Particular) Baptist Missionary Society
1795   London Missionary Society
1799   Church Missionary Society
since 1796 many American mission boards

The Postmillennialism of Spener, Francke and the Pietist Mission Work

None less than the 'Father' of German missiology, Gustav Warneck, considering the influence of eschatology on Reformed mission work, has also discovered that Lutheran eschatology hindered missions up to the rise of Pietism.[187] Luther believed that the world was soon to end[188] and that the apostles had already fulfilled the Great Commission.[189] Christianity waited for Christ's return, but "expects nothing from this earth."[190] This is true for Lutheran theology in general, as Helmuth Egelkraut has observed, "The

---

[187] Gustav Warneck, *Abriß einer Geschichte der protestantischen Missionen von der Reformation bis auf die Gegenwart* (Berlin: Martin Warneck, 1899), p. 10-18. See also: Helmut Eglkraut, *Die Zukunftserwartung der pietistischen Väter*, Theologie und Dienst 53 (Gießen: Brunnen Verlag, 1987), p. 11.

[188] Julius Köstlin, *Luthers Theologie in ihrer geschichtlichen Entwicklung und ihrem inneren Zusammenhange dargestellt*, vol. 2 (Stuttgart: J. F. Steinkopf, 1901²), pp. 335-340

[189] See Norman E. Thomas, ed., *Classic Texts in Mission and World Christianity*, American Society of Missiology Series 20 (Maryknoll, N. Y.: Orbis Books, 1995) pp. 33-35. This is also true of the Lutheran missiologist, Philipp Nicolai (1556-1608); see Ibid., pp. 43-46.

[190] Helmuth Egelkraut, *Die Zukunftserwartungen der pietistischen Väter*, Theologie und Dienst 53 (Brunnen Verlag: Gießen, 1987), p. 11, describing Luther's eschatology.

nearness of the end of the world is and remains the orthodox conviction, which is not to be shaken."[191]

The close tie between Postmillennialism, the Reformed doctrine of salvation, and the awakening of Evangelical missionary thought can be observed in the German Evangelical movement as well as in America and England. Also Philipp Jakob Spener (1633-1705), August Hermann Francke (1663-1727)[192] and other Pietist fathers of missions were Postmillennialists.

Spener, the 'Father of German Pietism', was Lutheran and Postmillennialist. Helmuth Egelkraut writes:

> "Should one wish to sort Spener into one of the common eschatological systems, one would have to consider him a Postmillennialist. But Spener refuses to set up a closed prophetic system."[193]

Many see the Reformed influences on Spener's eschatology (and in his different view of orthodox Lutheranism).[194] Thus, Carl Hinrichs says: "Pietism in Germany helped the Puritan type to come out."[195]

Spener's Postmillennialism inspired the first outbreak of Pietist-Lutheran world missions in the seventeenth century, particularly after the activity of August Hermann Francke, just as Puritan Postmillennialism inspired the beginning of Reformed world missions. "The enthusiasm for

---

[191] Ibid., p. 14. Will-Erich Peuckert, *Die große Wende: Geistesgeschichte und Volkskunde*, Vol. 2, (Darmstadt: Wissenschaftliche Buchgesellschaft, 1966), pp. 545-555, has shown, that Luther's eschatological view was based on medieval models.

[192] Iain Murray, *The Puritan Hope*, pp. 131-132. Murray wrongly adds Bengel, who will be dealt with later.

[193] Helmuth Egelkraut, *Die Zukunftserwartungen der pietistischen Väter*, op. cit., p. 27. Spener did not indeed wish to set up a 'system'. This does not stand in the way of a classification, for many representatives of the various systems did not define closed systems, and thus never classified themselves under any one school.

[194] See Wilhelm Goeters, *Die Vorbereitung des Pietismus in der reformierten Kirche der Niederlande bis zur labadistischen Krise 1670* (Leipzig; 1911); summarized by Johannes Wallmann, "Pietismus und Orthodoxie," *Zur neuren Pietismusforschung, Wege der Forschung* CDXL; ed. Martin Greschat (Darmstadt: Wissenschaftliche Buchgesellschaft,1977) pp. 53-81, here pp. 53-57.

[195] Carl Hinrichs, "Der Hallischen Pietismus als politisch-soziale Reformbewegung des 18 Jahrhunderts," *Zur neuren Pietismuforschung, Wege der Forschung* CDXL; ed. Martin Greschat (Darmstadt: Wissenschaftliche Buchgesellschaft,1977) pp. 243-258, here p. 252.

missions shown in the early nineteenth century arose from the same eschatological expectations."[196]

Spener's "Theological Thoughts" contain a short summary of his eschatological views.

> "That Popery and the Roman Babylon will be completely cast down before the end of the world, but that the Jewish people will be again converted through the grace of God, so that the knowledge of God will be gloriously increased, the Christian church transformed into a more holy and glorious condition and that thus the fulfillment of all other divine promises belonging to this time will come to pass, which I believe to be the thousand years of the Revelation of St. John. This doctrine, which is so firmly founded in Scripture, and is in the most part held by not only the ancient, but also our teachers ..."[197]

Not only are Spener's major works, "Pia desideria" (Pious Wishes) and "Theologisches Bedencken" (Theological Thoughts), determined by the expectation of a better future, but also his previous dissertation on Revelations 9:13-21[198] and his book "The Hope for Better Times in the Future"[199] of 1696.

Martin Schmidt has noted that Spener's Reform program can only be understood on the basis of his eschatological hope.[200] Johannes Wallman believes that one of Spener's two major issues is the substitution of the Chiliast expectation of a better future prior to the Second Coming for the Lutheran[201] Amillennialist expectation of Christ's immediate return.[202]

---

[196] Helmuth Egelkraut, *Die Zukunftserwartungen der pietistischen Väter*, op. cit., p. 43.

[197] Philipp Jakob Spener, *Theologische Bedencken*, 4 Parts in 2 Volumes, Vol. 3, (Halle, Germany: Verlegung des Waysen-Hauses, 1712-1715), pp. 965-966.

[198] "Behauptung der Hoffnung künfftiger Zeiten in Rettung des insgeheim gegen dieselbe unrecht geführten Spruches Luc XVIII vs 8" (1692/3), quoted by Helmuth Egelkraut, *Die Zukunftserwartungen der pietistischen Väter*, op. cit., p. 21.

[199] "Von der Hoffnung zukünftiger besserer Zeiten."

[200] Martin Schmidt, "Speners 'Pia Desideria': Versuch einer theologischen Interpretation," *Zur neueren Pietismusforschung*, op. cit., p. 113-166. See also Helmuth Egelkraut, *Die Zukunftserwartungen der pietistischen Väter*, op. cit., p. 16.

[201] Johannes Wallmann, "Vom Kathechismuschristentum zum Bibelchristentum", *Die Zukunft des Schriftprinzips, Bibel im Gespräch* 2, ed. Richart Ziegert (Stuttgart: Deutsche Bibelgesellschaft, 1994), pp. 34-38, 50. Wallmann also shows that whereas Luther held the catechism was essential to all, and substituted it for the Scriptures, Spener emphasized the use of whole Bible in church services and in the family, making the catechism merely a compendium for beginners.

"It is evident that Pietism won a new perspective on history, which lent it the scope necessary for that methodical, non-sectarian missionary affectivity, which we see in August Francke or Count Zinzendorf."[203]

Helmuth Egelkraut writes:

"The new element, the motor which gives its ideas power and drives it forward, is its eschatological center."[204]
"The time of God's great deeds is not in the past – as Orthodoxy believes – but in the future."[205]
"An activity long unknown broke out in German Protestantism."[206]

Erich Beyreuter states, "In his 'Behauptung der Hoffnung künftiger besserer Zeiten', Philipp Jacob Spener radically separates himself from the dark historical view of later Orthodoxy."[207]

Kurt Aland wants to refute this idea. Rather than Chiliasm, he believes that Spener taught the deferment of Christ's return by the conversion of the Jews and the fall of the Roman Church.[208] However, Aland fails to recognize that Spener did not believe that Christ would return immediately after these events, but that they would first introduce a period of better days. Wallman is correct when he writes about Spener, "The Scripture teaches a

---

[202] Johannes Wallmann, "Die Anfänge des Pietismus," *Jahrbuch der Geschichte des Pietismus* 4 (1979) pp. 11-53; Johannes Wallmann, *Der Pietismus. Die Kirche in ihrer Geschichte* 0/1 (Göttingen, Germany: Vandenhoeck & Ruprecht, 1990) pp 47-50; Johannes Wallmann, *Philipp Jakob Spener und die Anfänge des Pietismus, Beiträge zur historischen Theologie* 42 (Tübingen, Germany: 1986) pp. 307-335; Johannes Wallmann, "Pietismus und Chiliasmus: Zur Kontroverse um Philipp Jakob Speners 'Hoffnung besserer Zeiten,' *Zeitschrift für Theologie und Kirche* 78 (1981) pp. 235-266. See also Dietrich Blaufuß, "Zu Ph. J. Speners Chiliasmus und seinen Kritikern," *Pietismus und Neuzeit: Ein Jahrbuch zur Geschichte des neueren Protestantismus* 14 (1988); *Chiliasmus in Deutschland und England im 17. Jahrhundert*, pp. 85-108, which, however, does not believe Spener to have been a Chiliast.
[203] Johannes Wallmann, "Pietismus und Orthodoxie," op. cit., p. 80.
[204] Helmuth Egelkraut, *Die Zukunftserwartung der pietistischen Väter*," op. cit., p. 16.
[205] Ibid., p. 20.
[206] Ibid., p. 24.
[207] Erich Beyreuter, "Evangelische Missionstheologe im 16. und 17. Jahrhundert," *Evangelische Missions-Zeitschrift* 18 (1961) pp. 1-10, 33-43. (On Spener, see pp. 38-39. On Pietist criticism of Lutheran expectations of the immediate return of Christ, see pp. 39.)
[208] Kurt Aland, "Philipp Jakob Spener und die Anfänge des Pietismus," *Jahrbuch für die Geschichte des Pietismus* 4 (1979) pp. 155-189.

promised Kingdom of Christ on earth prior to the Last Judgment."[209] This is a classical definition of Postmillennial doctrine. Martin Greschat and Gerhard Maier rightly point out that Spener's hope of a better future is an element completely foreign to Lutheranism, an element which, along with the New Birth, was the leading idea of the new movement.[210] Erich Beyreuter writes:

> "Spener surprised his generation with his future expectations, which he had discovered in the New Testament ... He possessed with them the power, not to criticize the Lutheran orthodoxy, but to conquer it as an epoch."[211]

Peter Zimmerling expresses this achievement with the following words,

> "This Chiliast-nurtured hope for the future conquered the pessimism of orthodoxy from within."[212]

August Hermann Francke, the second generation leader of Pietism in Germany, shared Speners views to the most part[213], after Spener had helped him to give up his 'enthusiastic' "Chiliast expectations of the immediate return"[214] of Christ common to radical, spiritualist Pietism. Egelkraut writes about Francke:

> "The faith in the better days of the future, which Spener had rediscovered, proved to be a world – transforming power. Zinzendorf is also to be found in its magnetic field."[215]

---

[209] Johannes Wallman, *Der Pietismus*, op. cit., p. 49.
[210] See Martin Greschat, "Die 'Hoffnung bessere Zeiten' für die Kirche," *Zur neueren Pietismusforschung, Wege der Forschung* CDXL, ed. Martin Greschat (Darmstadt: Wissenschaftliche Buchgesellschaft, 1977), which includes good documentation. Gerhard Maier, *Die Johannesoffenbarung und die Kirche, Wissenschaftliche Untersuchungen zum Neuen Testament* 25 (Tübingen, Germany: J. C. B: Mohr, 1981) pp. 354-355. See pp. 353-366 on Spener's escatology.
[211] Erich Beyreuter, *Geschichte des Pietismus* (Stuttgart: J. F. Steinkopf, 1978) p. 95. See also Helmuth Egelkraut, *Die Zukunftserwartung der pietistischen Väter*, op. cit., p. 16-24.
[212] Peter Zimmerling, *Pioniere der Mission im älteren Pietismus, Theologie und Dienst* 47 (Gießen, Germany: Brunnenverlag, 1985) p. 11.
[213] Gerhard Maier, *Die Johannesoffenbarung und die Kirche*, op. cit., pp. 368-370, agrees that Francke's work can only be understood against the background of Spener's influence, but sees a certain extenuation of Spener's views in Francke's opinions.
[214] Johannes Wallmann, *Der Pietismus*, op. cit., p. 68.
[215] Helmut Egelkraut, *Die Zukunftserwartung der pietistischen Väter*, op. cit., p. 31.

> "Spener's vision of the future began to take shape: the mission to the Jews and to the heathen, the ministry to the poor and the dispossessed and that across denominational lines."[216]

And Zimmerling summarizes Francke's pedagogies, which led to the founding of many private Christian schools:

> "In his 'Greater Essay', Francke develops a thorough program for the raising and education of children, to effect a concrete improvement of the world."[217]

Egelkraut mentions that Francke communicated frequently with the members of the Society for the Promotion of Christian Knowledge in London and with Cotton Mather, a Calvinist in Boston,[218] thus maintaining contact and communication with Reformed, Postmillennialist mission groups. (Mather was the author of the well-known biography of John Elliot.)[219]

Friedhelm Groth has thoroughly traced in detail[220] the development of (Postmillennial) Chiliasm propagated by Spener and Francke to the Premillennialism of the Württemberg Pietism, which was closely related to Universalism.[221] Johann Albrecht Bengel (1687-1752) was the bond. He assumed two millennia, one in Rev. 20:1-3 and the other in 20:4-6.[222] The first of which corresponded to Spener's view, while the other postulated Christ's direct rule and contained all the elements typical of the Premillen-

---

[216] Ibid., p. 29. See also Carl Hinrichs, "Der Hallische Pietismus als politisch-soziale Reformbewegung des 18 Jahrhunderts," *Zur neueren Pietismusforschung*, ed. Martin Greschat, op. cit., pp. 243-258; Gerhard Bondi, "Der Beitrag des hallischen Pietismus zur Entwicklung des ökonomischen Denkens in Deutschland," *Zur neueren Pietismusforschung*, op. cit., pp. 259-293 (particularly pp. 268-269 on the influence of the Pietist work ethic).

[217] Peter Zimmerling, *Pioniere der Mission im älteren Pietismus*, op. cit., p. 16.

[218] Helmut Egelkraut, *Die Zukunftserwartung der pietistischen Väter*, op. cit., p. 29. A. de Jong, *As the Waters that Cover the Sea*, op. cit., discusses the correspondence of 1714 on p. 102-103, 107. According to Ibid., p. 85, Francke became a corresponding member of the S. P. C. K. in 1700.

[219] Iain Murray, *The Puritan Hope*, op. cit., p. 93.

[220] Friedhelm Groth, *Die "Wiederbringung aller Dinge" in württembergischen Pietismus, Arbeiten zur Geschichte des Pietismus* 21 (Göttingen, Germany: Vandenhoeck & Ruprecht, 1984).

[221] See also Gerhard Maier, *Die Johannesoffenbarung und die Kirche*, op. cit., pp. 367-447.

[222] Friedhelm Groth, *Die "Wiederbringung aller Dinge" in württembergischen Pietismus*, op. cit., pp. 72-74. See also Gerhard Maier, *Die Johannesoffenbarung und die Kirche*, op. cit., 432 (Maier considers this development positively); Iain Murray, *The Puritan Hope*, op. cit., p. 132, wrongly considers Bengel one of the fathers of Postmillennial Pietism.

nial view and the 'Restoration of all things".[223] The latter was a view opposite of Spener's.[224]

Rufus Anderson

More than others, Rufus Anderson (1796-1880), the American mission leader, embodies the continuing ties between Calvinist Soteriology, Postmillennialism and active world missions a generation after Carey. After leading the oldest and largest American missionary society for decades, he accepted a position as professor of missiology at Andover Theological Seminary, the world's first chair for missiology.[225] The German *Lexikon zur Weltmission* calls him the "most influential figure in American missions".[226] R. Pierce Beaver writes, that until the Second World War, all American Protestant missionaries owed at least lip service to Anderson's goals.[227] He exerted immeasurable influence on important leaders in world missions, such as Roland Allen, Robert E. Speer, John Nevius,[228] Abraham Kuyper[229] and others.

In spite of his emphasis on the importance of the local church, Rufus, a Calvinist and a Congregationalist, taught the importance of evangelizing the heathen, because, as a Postmillennialist, he expected the conversion of whole nations.[230] R. Pierce Beaver is correct in deriving Rufus' major mo-

---

[223] Friedhelm Groth, *Die "Wiederbringung aller Dinge" in württembergischen Pietismus*, op. cit., pp. 76-88.

[224] See Helmut Egelkraut, *Die Zukunftserwartung der pietistischen Väter*, op. cit., pp. 31-33.

[225] Thomas Schirrmacher, *Theodor Christlieb und seine Missionstheologie* (Wuppertal, Germany: Verlag der Evangelischen Gesellschaft für Deutschland, 1985) pp. 14-15.

[226] R. Pierce Beaver, "Rufus Anderson," *Lexikon zur Weltmission*, ed. Stephen Neill, (Wuppertal/Erlangen, Germany: Brockhaus/Verlag, 1975), p. 27.

[227] R. Pierce Beaver, *To Advance the Gospel: Selections from the Writings of Rufus Anderson* (Grand Rapids: Eerdmans, 1967), pp. 9-10.

[228] R. Pierce Beaver, "The Legacy of Rufus Anderson," *Occasional Bulletin of Missionary Research* 3 (1979) pp. 94-97, here pp. 96-97.

[229] Jan Verkuyl, *Contemporary Mission: An Introduction*, (Grand Rapids: Wm. B. Eerdmans, 1978) pp. 187 on Kuyper and the Netherlands.

[230] Thomas Schirrmacher ed., *Die Zeit für die Bekehrung der Welt ist reif: Rufus Anderson und die Selbständigkeit der Kirche als Ziel der Mission*, Edition afem: mission scripts 3 (Bonn: Verlag für Kultur und Wissenschaft, 1993) [German selection of works by and on Rufus Anderson]. See particularly, Thomas Schirrmacher, "Rufus Anderson und die Selbständigkeit der einheimischen Kirche: Auch ein Beitrag zum Verhältnis Glaubensmissionen und reformatorischen Bekenntnis," pp. 9-36, and Anderson's Postmillennial sermon, "The Time for the World's Conver-

tivation for missions to the greater motive of love of Christ rather than to his Postmillennial expectations[231]. Nevertheless, this was only possible due to the prevailing Postmillennial attitudes in the U.S.A. at the time[232], naturally shared by Anderson, as demonstrated in two smaller works, "Promised Advent of the Spirit" and "Time for the World's Conversion Come".[233]

Postmillennialism and The Great Commission Today

One of the most quoted verses in the Postmillennialist camp, nowadays as in Carey's time, is the Great Commission in Matthew 28:18-20.[234] For Postmillennialists this text teaches that evangelization and conversion have to come first, but have to also lead to a change in life-style and society through the keeping of divine Law. Above all, the Postmillennialist interpretation, in contrast to other explanations, sees these verses not only as a commission, but also as prophecy[235]: Jesus' commandment will become reality. This reality is that one day all people will be converted and will keep God's Law. Kenneth L. Gentry, the author of a Postmillennial book about the Great Commission and the usual contemporary representation of Postmillennialism writes the following about the relationship between the Great Commission and Postmillennialism,

---

sion of the World Come", pp. 115-128. See also R. Pierce Beaver, *To Advance the Gospel: Selections from the Writings of Rufus Anderson*.

[231] R. Pierce Beaver, "Eschatology in American Missions," *Basileia: Walter Freytag zum 60. Geburtstag*, ed. Jan Heremlink, Hans Jochen Margul (Stuttgart: Evangelischer Missionsverlag, 1959) pp. 60-75, here p. 70.

[232] Ibid., p. 60-75; Peter Kawerau, *Amerika und die orientalischen Kirchen: Ursprung und Anfang der amerikanischen Mission unter den Nationalkirchen Westasiens*, op. cit., pp. 624-629.

[233] Ibid. pp. 624-629 includes detailed discussion of Anderson's Postmillennialism. See the text in pp. 70-72 and the complete texts in R. Pierce Beaver, *To Advance the Gospel: Selections from the Writings of Rufus Anderson*, op. cit., p. 45-70.

[234] See Kenneth L. Gentry, *The Greatness of the Great Commission* (Tyler, Texas: Institute for Christian Economics, 1990). See also the older version in the *Journal of Christian Reconstruction* 7 (Winter/1981) Vol. 2, Symposium on Evangelism, pp. 19-47; Greg L. Bahnsen, "The Prima Facie Acceptability of Postmillennialism," op. cit., pp. 48-105; Mark M. Kreitzer, "God's Plan for Christian South Africa: Dominion and Missions" (Capetown, Pretoria: Conference for Christian Action, 1990).

[235] This idea can sometimes be found in nonreformed and premillennial writings, e.g. Millard J. Erickson, *Christian Theology*, one volume edition (Grand Rapids, Mich.: Baker Book House, 1990) p. 1207.

"note, that the postmillennial view is the only one of the three major evangelical eschatologies that builds its case on the very charter for Christianity, the Great Commission (Matt. 28:18-20)."[236]

Gentry bases his statement on one of the leading Postmillennialists of the last century, the Scottish Presbyterian theologian David Brown,[237] who built his eschatology on the Great Commission. He also bases his statement on a Dispensationalist theologian, Charles C. Ryrie, who criticized the expectation of the Postmillennialists. He believed that, "The Great Commission will be fulfilled."[238]

Even today, there are Reformed denominations, such as the Free Presbyterian Church of Scotland[239] or the Reformed Presbyterian Church in the United States,[240] that think completely in Postmillennial terms and derive their eschatology from the Great Commission.

Jordan has demonstrated that until 1930, almost all leading theologians and mission leaders of southern Presbyterianism were Postmillennialists.[241] The leading theologians of Princeton Theological Seminary, including Benjamin B. Warfield,[242] were Postmillennialists, as well. John Jefferson Davis writes, "I was struck by the fact that postmillennialism, now almost forgotten in conservative circles, was for much of the nineteenth century the dominant millennial understanding".[243]

---

[236] Kenneth L. Gentry, *He Shall Have Dominion: A Postmillennial Eschatology* (Tyler, Texas: Institute for Christian Economics, 1992) p. 223.

[237] Ibid, pp. 233-234 on David Brown, *Christ's Second Coming: Will it Be Premillennial?* (1887, repr. St. Edmonton, Canada: Still Waters Revival Books, 1990) p. 298.

[238] Charles C. Ryrie, *Basic Theology* (Wheaton, Ill: Victor, 1986) p. 441. Cited by Kenneth L. Gentry, *He Shall Have Dominion*, op.cit., p. 234; similar Millard J. Erickson, *Christian Theology*, op.cit., p. 1206.

[239] D. MacLeod, "The Millennium," *Free Presbyterian Magazine* 96 no. 8 (Edinburgh: Aug. 1991), p. 261-268; Lachlan MacKenzie, "The Millennium," *Free Presbyterian Magazine* 97 no. 10 (Edinburgh: Oct. 1992) pp. 305-309.

[240] "The Reformed Presbyterian Church in the United States. A Church Burning with Vision" (Atlanta, Ga.: The Reformed Presbyterian Church in the United States).

[241] James B. Jordan, "A Survey of Sourthern Presbyterian Millennial Views Before 1930", The Journal of Christain Reconstruction 3, no. 2 (1976/1977) pp. 106-121. Compare Morton H. Smith, *Studies in Southern Presbyterian Theology* (Phillipsburg, N. J.: Presbterian & Reformed Publ., 1987) pp. 180-181.

[242] Benjamin Warfield, "The Millennium and the Apocalypse," The Princeton Theological Review 2 (1904) pp. 599-617. Repr. Benjamin Warfield, *Biblical Doctrines*, (1929, repr. Edinburgh: The Banner of Truth Trust, 1988) pp. 643-664.

[243] John Jefferson Davis, *Christ's Victorious Kingdom: Postmillennialism Reconsidered* (Grand Rapids: Baker Book House, 1986) p. 7, 10.

In 1909, W.O. Carver observed that the Postmillennial view was the most common motivation for missions.[244] This remained the case until the end of the First World War.

Was Calvin a Postmillennialist?

John Jefferson Davis observes that Calvin assumed that true religion and the glory of Christ's dominion would spread over the whole earth,[245] as he had repeated in numerous sermons and commentaries, as well as in his dedication of the *Institutes* to Francis I of France. Jefferson adds, "Calvin's outlook does not, of course, represent a fully articulated postmillennialism, but does foreshadow subsequent developments."[246] Positively stated, Davis says, "John Calvin ... had an understanding of the kingship of Christ that paved the way for the full flowering of the postmillennial view in English Puritanism."[247]

Iain Murray shares this view and demonstrates that Calvin, in contrast to Luther, expected a great future for the Kingdom of God.[248] Charles L. Chaney also assumes that the Puritans, as well as Jonathan Edwards, built their Postmillennialism on Calvin's eschatology.[249] Calvin, says Chaney, had been familiar with the three steps of salvation history, the Age of the Apostles, the Age of the Antichrist (Calvin's day) and the Age of the Expansion of the Church among all peoples, whereby the Gospel would reach various nations at different times, according to divine election.[250]

Walter Nigg, describing Calvin's eschatology, writes:

> "Seeing the Kingdom of God in history is the new *motif* in Calvin's understanding of divine dominion. The Kingdom is not to be expected in its completion in the near future, it is in a state of development, in a mighty battle with the powers of Darkness."[251]

In his belief that the Kingdom of God is involved in an historical wrestling match, Calvin implies that salvation history is closely bound to political

---

[244] W. O. Carver, "The Missionary Consummation-Prophecy of Missions," *Mission in the Plan of the Ages* (New York: Revell, 1909), pp. 213-282.
[245] John Jefferson Davis, *Christ's Victorious Kingdom*, op. cit., pp. 16-17.
[246] Ibid. p. 17
[247] Ibid. p. 16
[248] Iain Murray, *The Puritan Hope*, op. cit., pp. 40-41.
[249] Charles L. Chaney, *The Birth of Missions in America*, op. cit., pp. 32-35.
[250] Ibid., p. 270.
[251] Walter Nigg, *Das ewige Reich* (Berlin: Gebrüder Weiss, n d.), pp. 32-35.

events and hints at a definite "progressive" opinion.²⁵² Heinrich Berger has shown that Calvin did not express an expectation of the immediate return of Christ.²⁵³

David E. Holwerda considers Calvin an Amillennialist,²⁵⁴ opposing Millennialist views. This is because he assumed that since the Kingdom of God is already present in Christ, His rule on earth would be invisible.²⁵⁵ Holwerda adds that this idea does not, however, contradict Postmillennial interpretation,

> "But Calvin believes that the perfected kingdom already exists in Christ, that it is eternal and includes the renovation of the world. Consequently, Christ's visible appearance can mean only the final revelation of the perfected kingdom."²⁵⁶

Georg Huntemann writes in his homage to Calvin's view, ²⁵⁷

> "The Millennium had, in the Reformation, experienced progress, had gone into action. Not only the Church, but the complete world order was to be brought into line with divine order."²⁵⁸

The premillennialist Millard J. Erickson proved that Reformed thinking theologians of all times, such as Augustin, Calvin, and Warfield, have been claimed for the amillennial as well as the postmillennial camp²⁵⁹, which for him is not by chance, as both views cannot be clearly separated from each other. Nevertheless for him, those theologians belong to the postmillennial camp, because with true amillennialists (e.g. Lutheran theologians) the problem of being claimed for two camps never arose.

---

²⁵² Ibid., p. 229.
²⁵³ Heinrich Berger, *Calvins Geschichtsauffassung, Studien zur Dogmengeschichte und Systematischen Theologie* (Zürich, Switzerland: Zwingli Verlag, 1956), pp- 74-77.
²⁵⁴ David E. Howerda, "Eschatology and History: A Look at Calvin's Eschatological Vision," *Readings in Calvin's Theology*, ed. Donald K. McKim (Grand Rapids: Baker Book House, 1984) pp. 311-342. Also in *Calvin's Theology, Theology Proper, Eschatology. Articles on Calvin and Calvinism* Vol. 9, ed. Richard C. Gamble (New York/London: Garland, 1992) pp. 130-160.
²⁵⁵ David E. Howerda, "Eschatology and History: A Look at Calvin's Eschatological Vision," op. cit., p. 311-342.
²⁵⁶ Ibid., p. 329
²⁵⁷ Georg Huntemann, *Der verlorene Maßstab: Gottes Gebot im Chaos dieser Zeit* (Bad Liebenzell: Verlag der Liebenzeller Mission, 1983), pp. 131-135.
²⁵⁸ Ibid., p. 131.
²⁵⁹ Millard J. Erickson, *Christian Theology*, op. cit., p. 1212.

Premillennialism originally opposed to missions

The dissemination of Postmillennialism demonstrates the conflicts which developed with the growth of Premillennialism. John Nelson Darby, founder of Dispensationalism[260], expresses the Premillennial view of missions in a 1840 lecture in Geneva,

> "I am afraid that many a cherished feeling, dear to the children of God, has been shocked this evening; I mean their hope that the gospel will spread by itself over the whole earth during the actual dispensation."[261]

The influential Pietist professor of Systematic Theology in Tübingen, Johann Tobias Beck (1804-1878), opposed the work of the Basel Mission and the spreading evangelical world mission movement in general. His objection was that Jesus must first return, so that missions would be carried out and succeed in the Millennium.[262] Theodor Oehler[263] and Hermann Gundert, representatives of the Basel Mission, confronted this opinion with a Postmillennial[264] reply, although using different terms[265].

---

[260] See the definition in Thomas Schirrmacher, Hans-Georg Wünch, Stephan Zehnle, "Nachwort über die darbystische Lehre vom Dispensationalismus", John F. Walvoord, Roy F. Zuck ed., *Das Alte Testament erklärt und ausgelegt. Bd. 1. 1. Mose – 2. Samuel* (Neuhausen: Hänssler, 1985), pp. 607-608. The best work on the theology of Darby is, to my knowledge, Erich Geldbach, *Christliche Versammlung und Heilsgeschichte bei John Nelson Darby* (Wuppertal: Brockhaus, 1975³).

[261] *The Collected Writings of J. N. Darby. Prophetic*, Vol. 1, cited by Iain Murray, *The Puritan Hope*, op. cit., p. 186.

[262] See Thomas Schirrmacher, *Theodor Christlieb und seine Missionstheologie*, op. cit., pp. 34-36 and the literature listed in note 30, page 36; Helmut Egelkraut, *Die Zukunftserwartung der pietistischen Väter*, op. cit., pp. 44-45.

[263] Theodor Oehler, *Die Mission und die Zukunft des Reiches Gottes*, Basler Missions-Studien 10 (Basel: Verlag der Missionsbuchhandlung, 1902), pp.4-6 (contra Beck and his influential sermon of 1850).

[264] Ibid., pp. 8-10, esp. 9, demonstrates Oehler's Postmillennial view very clearly.

[265] This view is also taken by Helmut Egelkraut, *Die Zukunftserwartung der pietistischen Väter*, op. cit., pp. 40-43; compare with the postmillennialism of the Basel Mission: Christine Schirrmacher, *Mit den Waffen des Gegners: Christlich-Muslimische Kontroversen im 19. und 20. Jahrhundert*, Islamkundliche Untersuchungen 162 (Berlin: Klaus Schwarz Verlag, 1992), pp. 33-34 with examples from the *Evangelischen Missionsmagazin*, the Journal of the Basel Mission, in the years 1826 and 1832. Both the founders Christian Friedrich Spittler (1782-1867) and his colleague, Nikolaus von Brunn (1766-1849), the pastor in Basel, already showed Postmillennial tendencies, see Helmuth Egelkraut, *Die Zukunftserwartung der pietistischen Väter*, op. cit., pp. 40-43.

Oehler, however, experienced a change of opinion about the relationship between Premillennialism and missions. Whereas Premillennialism was an argument against hopes of evangelistic success for Darby and Beck, Premillennialist faith missions became one of the major mainsprings of the world's missions. Oehler describes the contrast between Beck and the new mission movements, ("For these, the expectation of Christ's immediate return has become the strongest motivation for missions."[266]) but remarks critically,

> "Here I must protest against the assertion of the Alliance Mission, namely the assumption that it is our business to hasten Christ's return by our missionary activity."[267]

2.2. Carey's Postmillennialism

Postmillennialism in the "Enquiry"

Let us examine the central indications of Carey's Postmillennialism in the 'Enquiry". Carey had two questions to answer about the Great Commission: 1. Was the Great Commission directed only to the apostles or is it valid for all Christians of all eras? 2. Can the Great Commission be fulfilled?

Answering the first question, Carey points out that the Great Commission is binding "even to the end of the age." (Mt. 28:20)[268] One of his best arguments for the validity of the Commission is the fact that it includes the command to baptize that all churches and theologians consider valid.[269] If the Great Commission was directed only to the apostles, churches would have to stop baptizing people.

The answer to the second question arises from Carey's Postmillennial expectation of missions' final success. Premillennialism, which molded Post-Classical missions, did not assume such achievement, but only the conversion of a minority from each nation.

In his introduction, Carey expresses no doubts that God would build his kingdom on this earth to the same extent as the devil's present government:

> "Yet God repeatedly made known his intention to prevail finally over all the power of the devil, and to destroy all his works and set up his own kingdom

---

[266] Theodor Oehler, *Die Mission und die Zukunft des Reiches Gottes*, op. cit., p. 6
[267] Ibid. p. 11.
[268] William Carey, "Enquiry", p. 9.
[269] Ibid., p. 9. See also James R. Beck, *Dorothy Carey*, op. cit., p. 63.

and interest among men, and extend it as universally as Satan had extended his."[270]

Very early in the "Enquiry" Carey refutes objections to the continuing validity of the Great Commission on eschatological grounds:

"It has been said that some learned divines have proved from Scripture that the time is not yet come that the heathen should be converted; and that first the witnesses must be slain,[271] and many other prophecies fulfilled. But admitting this to be the case (which I much doubt[272]) yet, if any objection is made from this against preaching to them immediately, it must be founded on one of these things; either that the secret purpose of God is the rule of our duty, and then it must be as bad to pray for them, as to preach to them; or else that none shall be converted in the heathen world till the universal down pouring of the Spirit in the last days. But this objection comes too late; for the success of the gospel has been very considerable in many places already."[273]

On one hand, he questions his own eschatological view, while on the other, he objects to any interpretation which prohibits the present carrying out of the Great Commission.[274] The Christian must make his decisions not according to the unknown mysteries of God's will but according to His clear, revealed commandment. Carey here follows Calvin's distinction between God's sovereign will, Providence, and His moral will, which is our duty.[275]

Carey drew his argument against the predominate view of the day, that the witness must first be slain, from Jonathan Edward's detailed discussion.[276]

---

[270] William Carey, "Enquiry", p. 5.
[271] Rev. 11:7.
[272] (Footnote by Carey:) See Edwards on Prayer, on this subject lately re-printed by Mr. Sutcliffe.
[273] William Carey, "Enquiry", p. 12.
[274] Compare the view outlined below, of Johann Tobias Beck, a few years later.
[275] See Johannes Calvin, *Unterricht in der christlichen Religion: Institutio Religionis Christianae* (Neukirchen, Germany: 1988) p. 129 (1st Book, Chapter 18, Paragraph 4) and p. 234f; similar Francis Turretin, *Institutes of Elenctic Theology*, ed. by James T. Dennison, vol. 1 (Phillipsburg, NJ: Presbyterian & Reformed, 1992) pp. 220-222 and Thomas Schirrmacher, *Ethik* Vol. 1 (Neuhausen, Germany: Hänssler, 1994), pp. 723-732.
[276] Jonathan Edwards, *The Works of Jonathan Edwards*, Vol. 2 (1834/1974, repr. Edinburgh: The Banner of Truth Trust, 1992) pp. 278-315). See also Peter Kawerau, *Amerika und die orientalischen Kirchen*, op. cit., pp. 72-73.

The other argument that Carey would have accepted against missions would have been the lack of converts in the heathen world. This, however, was refuted by reality. Interestingly, Carey fails to mention the expectation of the universal pouring out of the Holy Spirit, which was to initiate the great conversion of the heathen, which was, after all, his own opinion. Because this view also could be used against missions, he emphasized the role of the Great Commission as a commandment rather than eschatological opinions as the basis of our plans and actions.

Towards the end of the "Enquiry" Carey defines his eschatological view more clearly, but the complete picture becomes clear only in the light of the Postmillennial views of the day. Carey emphasizes that the prophesied growth of the Kingdom of God should not make the believer passive, but increases the obligation to missions.

> "If the prophecies concerning the increase of Christ's kingdom are true, and if what has been advanced concerning the commission given by him to his disciples being obligatory on us, be just, it must be inferred that all Christians ought heartily to concur with God in promoting his glorious designs for he that is joined to the Lord is one spirit."[277]

At the same time, he sees the first signs of the approaching expansion of the Kingdom of God in the social and political arena, but foremost, in the open doors.

> "... yea, a glorious door is opened, and is likely to be opened wider and wider, by the spread of civil and religious liberty, accompanied also by a diminution of the spirit of popery; a noble effort has been made to abolish the inhuman Slave-Trade, and though at present it has not been so successful as might be wished, yet it is hoped it will be preserved in, till it is accomplished."[278]

In Carey's view, Biblical eschatology does not refute God's commandments, but supports them. Thus, while discussing future promises, he can also allude to Christian responsibility and failure.

> "If an holy solicitude had prevailed in all the assemblies of Christians in behalf of their Redeemer's kingdom, we might probably have seen before now, not only an open door[279] for the gospel, but many running to and fro, and

---

[277] Carey, "Enquiry", p. 79.
[278] Ibid., p. 79.
[279] Rev. 3:20.

knowledge increased[280]; or a diligent use of those means which providence has put in our power, accompanied with a greater blessing than ordinary from heaven."[281]

Carey' interpretation of Zecharia was inspired by Jonathan Edward's[282] interpretation, which was popular at the time.

> "It is as represented in the prophets, that when there shall be a great mourning in the land, as the mourning of Hadadrimmon in the valley of Megiddon, and every family shall mourn apart, and their wives apart, it shall all follow upon a spirit of grace, and supplication.[283] And when these things shall take place, it is promised that there shall be a fountain opened for the house of David, and for the inhabitants of Jerusalem, for sin and for uncleanness,[284] – and that the idols shall be destroyed[285] and the false prophets ashamed of their profession.[286] Zech. xii. 10.14. – xiii. 1.6. This prophesy seems to teach that when there shall be a universal conjunction in fervent prayer, and all shall esteem Zion's welfare as their own, then copious influences of the Spirit shall be shed upon the churches, which like a purifying fountain shall cleanse the servants of the Lord. Nor shall this cleansing influence stop here; all old idolatrous prejudices shall be rooted out, and truth will prevail so gloriously that false teachers shall be so ashamed as rather to wish to be classed with obscure herdsmen, or the meanest peasants, than bear the ignominy attendant on their detection.
>
> The most glorious works of grace that have ever taken place have been in answer to prayer. It is in this way, we have the greatest reason to suppose, that the glorious out-pouring of the Spirit, which we expect at last, will be bestowed."[287]

In the "Enquiry", Carey not only thinks and argues from a Postmillennialist position, but also finds his examples among Postmillennialist missionaries and theologians. The Calvinist (Puritan) missionaries mentioned as examples[288] in the second and third chapters were missionaries to the

---

[280] Dan. 12:4.
[281] Ibid., p. 80.
[282] See Brian Stanley, *The History of the Baptist Missionary Society 1792-1992*, op. cit., p. 13 and Frank Deauville Walker, *William Carey*, op. cit., p. 59.
[283] Zech. 12:11; 10:14.
[284] Zech. 13:1.
[285] Zech. 13:2.
[286] Zech. 13:4.
[287] Carey, "Enquiry", p. 78-79.
[288] Carey. "Enquiry", p. 35, 69, 70.

Indians, John Eliot (1604-1690)[289] and David Brainerd (1718-1747).[290] Carey's original models[291] came too from the sphere of Jonathan Edward's influence. They both were Postmillennialists[292] and believed that numerous conversions would occur at the end of time, i.e., at the beginning of the Millennium, prior to Christ's return. (Carey read and continually re-read Edward's post mortem biography of Brainerd, not only in England but also later in India.)[293]

The Postmillennialist,[294] John Edwards, the Calvinist evangelist and the leading American theologian of his day, called for a world-wide prayer chain for world missions in his pamphlet, "A Humble Attempt to Promote Explicit Agreement and Visible Union Among God's People in Extraordinary Prayer for the Revival of Religion and the Advancement of Christ's Kingdom on Earth".[295] In referring to this work in the "Enquiry",[296] Carey

---

[289] See Wolf-Christian Jaeschke, "Der Indianermissionar John Eliot (1604-1698): Sein Denken und Wirken nach den 'Magnalia Christi Americana", *Evangelikale Missiologie* 9 (1993) 1: 3-12; Gustav Warneck, *Abriß einer Geschichte der protestantischen Missionen von der Reformation bis auf die Gegenwart*, op. cit., p. 46. On Eliot's Postmillennialist views, see Sidney H. Rooy, *The Theology of Missions in the Puritan Tradition*, op. cit., pp. 224-229; Neville B. Cryer, "John Eliot", *Five Pioneer Missionaries* (London: The Banner of Truth Trust, 1965) pp. 171-231.

[290] See on Brainerd's theology and postmillennialism Norman Petit, "Editor's Introduction" to *The Life of David Brainerd*, by Jonathan Edwards, op. cit., pp. 24-70; John Thornbury, "David Brainerd", *Five Pioneer Missionaries*, op. cit., pp. 13-91.

[291] See Ernest A. Payne, "Two Dutch Translations by Carey: An Angus Library Find", *The Baptist Quarterly* NS 11 (1942) pp. 33-38; James R. Beck, *Dorothy Carey*, op. cit., pp. 53-59; Harald Schilling, "Der geistige und geistliche Werdegang William Careys ... ", op. cit., pp. 85-86. Schilling mentions also the writings by and on Bartholomäus Ziegenbalg (1682-1719) and his colleague in Tranquebar, India, Heinrich Plütschau (1677-1746), as an influence on Carey. This influence cannot, however, be as well demonstrated, although Carey mentions Ziegenbalg.

[292] See W. O. Carver, *Missions in the Plan of the Ages*, op. cit., pp. 213-282; Iain Murray, *The Puritan Hope*, op. cit., pp. 93-103.

[293] See See Frank Deauville Walker, *William Carey*, op. cit., p. 136 and James R. Beck, *Dorothy Carey*, op. cit., pp. 58.

[294] See C. C. Goen, "Jonathan Edwards: A New Departure in Eschatology", op. cit.; and on Edwards postmillennialism Sidney Rooy, *The Theology of Missions in the Puritan Tradition: A Study of Representative Puritans*, op. cit. The missionary awareness of Edwards and of the evangelistic, missionary movement he led is well depicted in Peter Kawerau, *Amerika und die orientalischen Kirchen*, op. cit., pp. 1-176.

[295] Boston, 1748; printed in *The Works of Jonathan Edwards*, Vol. 2 (1834/1974; repr. Edinburgh: Banner of Truth Trust, 1992) pp. 278-315.

mentions the British edition provided by John Sutcliffe in 1789, which together with the American edition of 1747 had strongly influenced the Baptists of Northumberland since 1784.[297] In his arguments for Postmillennial hope in the "Enquiry", Carey sometimes used the same scripture quotations as Edwards, particularly those from Zecharia.[298]

Besides Edwards, Eliot and Brainerd, the "Enquiry" also mentions the seaman, James Cook (1721-1779),[299] whose logbook he had studied diligently.[300] Cook's last voyage, partly described in his logbook of 1779, was published in 1784, and in 1785, reprinted by the *Northampton Mercury* in a series of pamphlets.[301] Carey writes, "My attention to missions was first awakened after I was at Moulton, by reading the Last Voyage of Captain Cook."[302]

Carey also became aware of the immense possibilities for missions of the new expeditions in the geographical descriptions of the *Northampton Mercury*, one of the oldest English weekly newspapers.[303] Without question, world wide exploration and the new possibilities for travel inspired Postmillennialism as much as the rising of Protestant world missions did.

---

[296] See Ernst A. Payne, "Carey's 'Enquiry': An Essay for the Ter-Jubilee", *International Review of Missions* 31 (1942) pp. 180-186; and Peter Kawerau, *Amerika und die orientalischen Kirchen*, op. cit., pp. 72-73.

[297] Ernest A. Payne, "Introduction", in: William Carey, *An Enquiry into the Obligations of Christians to Use Means for the Conversion of the Heathens* (London: The Carey Kingsgate Press: 1961) pp. i-xx, here pp. xii-xiii; James R. Beck, *Dorothy Carey*, op.cit., pp. 59-60 and Frank Deauville Walker, *William Carey*, op. cit., pp. 58-59; cf. Iain Murray, *The Puritan Hope*, op. cit., pp. 151-152.

[298] Frank Deaville Walker, *William Carey*, op. cit., p. 59.

[299] Carey, "Enquiry", p. 63.

[300] Frank Deaville Walker, *William Carey*, op. cit., pp. 49-50; James R. Beck, *Dorothy Carey*, op. cit., pp. 53-59; Harald Schilling, "Der geistige und geistliche Werdegang William Careys bis zu seiner Veröffentlichung der Enquiry im Jahr 1782", *Fundierte Theologische Abhandlungen Nr. 5* (Wuppertal, Germany: Verlag der Evangelischen Gesellschaft für Deutschland, 1987) pp. 85-86; Ernst A. Payne, "Introduction", "Enquiry" by William Carey, op. cit., pp. i-xx; Ernest A. Payne, "Two Dutch Translations by Carey: An Angus Library Find", op. cit.; W. Bieder, "William Carey 1761-1834", op. cit., p. 158.

[301] Frank Deaville Walker, *William Carey*, op. cit., p. 50.

[302] Ibid., p. 49.

[303] Frank Deaville Walker, *William Carey*, op. cit., pp. 22-23, 50-51; Ernst A. Payne, "Introduction", op. cit., p. xii. Walker's bibliography was the first to examine the significance of the *Northampton Mercury* for Carey's development. See also Kellsye Finnie, *William Carey*, op. cit., p. 16.

Not only Carey, but also his mission society and his team were Postmillennialists. A. Christopher Smith, writing about Carey, his colleague John Marshman and their representative at home, says:

> "In mission theology, the Serampore Fraternity[304] members were at the fore in declaring that the world would be evangelized properly only after the Holy Spirit was poured forth. Rufus Anderson was perhaps even more sanguine and triumphalist in his millennialist expectations."[305]

The significance of Postmillennialism (and of the Calvinist doctrine of predestination) can also be seen in another aspect: "Another remarkable feature of the Enquiry is that the argument of 'perishing heathen' is never used."[306]

Carey believed that the heathen were lost without Christ. He builds his arguments for missions, however, on positive ideas rather than on negative ones, which strongly distinguishes him from other methods of supporting missions.

3. Carey's Calvinism

Carey's Calvinism

Carey was a Protestant by conviction, as the anti-Catholic and anti-Papist tenor of his history of the church clearly demonstrates.[307] The turning point, he believed, was reached by the Reformers.[308] He names especially Luther, Calvin, Melanchthon, Bucer and Peter Martyr.[309] He held the true Protestant dogma as essential for missions and to the missionary, for missionaries must, among other things, be "of undoubted orthodoxy in their sentiments."[310]

---

[304] i. e.: Carey, Marshman and Anderson.
[305] A. Christopher Smith, "The Edinburgh Connection: Between the Serampore Mission and Western Missiology", *Missiology: An International Review* 18 (1990) 2 pp. 185-209.
[306] Aalbertinus Hermen Oussoren, *William Carey, Especially his Missionary Principles*, op. cit., p. 129.
[307] Carey, "Enquiry", op. cit., p. 33-36. E. Daniel Potts describes the anti-Catholic attitude of the Serampore team in *British Baptist Missionaries in India 1793-1837*, op. cit.
[308] Carey, "Enquiry", op. cit., p. 35.
[309] An Italian theologian influenced by Bucer, who in turn influenced the Calvinist nature of the English Reformation.
[310] Carey, "Enquiry", op. cit., p. 75.

Carey's theology is not only unusual for modern tastes in its Postmillennialism, but also in its Calvinist soteriology, for many now believe that the doctrine of predestination is extinguishing missionary effort rather than intensifying it. Carey, like most other Protestant missionaries and missionary leaders of his day, agreed with the Calvinist view.[311]

Up into our century, the English Baptists were divided into two groups, the Arminian 'General Baptists' and the Calvinist 'Particular Baptists',[312] to which John Bunyan and C. H. Spurgeon belonged.[313] The designations indicate the extent of Jesus' atoning death: 'General Baptists' believe that Jesus died for all, 'Particular Baptists' believe that He died only for the Elect.[314] Carey's Calvinist viewpoint is clearly demonstrated in various parts of his book.

Carey was not influenced by the Methodism of his day, as one might expect,[315] but as a Calvinist,[316] his significance lies in his reconciliation between the theology of the Reformation, particularly Reformed theology, and the Church's responsibility for missions. Frank Deauville Walker writes,

> "He could not harmonize the views of the hyper-Calvinists with the duty of calling men to Christ. On the other hand, the opposite doctrine of Arminia-

---

[311] See Andrew C. Ross, "Missionary Expansion", in *Encyclopedia of the Reformed Faith*, ed. Donald K. McKim (Louisville, Ky: Westminster\John Knox Press and Edinburgh: Saint Andrew Press, 1992) pp. 242-244.

[312] Carey, "Enquiry", op. cit., p. 84 (Carey uses this term for his own denomination.)

[313] Compare with Spurgeon's journal, *Sword and Trowel*, or with the journal of the Calvinist Baptists, *Reformation Today*, which is printed in Liverpool (See Nr. 95 Jan./Feb. 1987).

[314] See Thomas Schirrmacher, *Ethik*, Vol. 1 (Neuhausen, Germany: Hänssler Verlag, 1994) pp. 646-654; and Thomas Schirrmacher, *Römerbrief*, op. cit., pp. 252-256 for a chart showing the differences between the two views. Aalbertinus Hermen Oussoren, *William Carey, Especially his Missionary Principles*, op. cit., pp. 124-127, discusses the teachings of the Particular Baptists and the significance of their confession, the 'London Confession of Faith', a Baptist version of the Calvinist Westminster Confession. For a modern version, see; *The Baptist Confession of Faith 1689 with Scripture Proofs*, Updated with notes by Peter Masters (London: The Wakeman Trust, 1989). See also a modern commentary by Samuel E. Waldron, *A Modern Exposition of the 1689 Baptist Confession of Faith* (Durham: Evangelical Press, 1989). Cf. on the Particular Baptists Raymond Brown, *The English Baptists of the Eigteenth Century* (London: Baptist Historical Society, 1986) pp. 115-141.

[315] Frank Deauville Walker, *William Carey*, op. cit., pp. 35-36. Carey mentions Wesley only briefly in the "Enquiry" on p. 37.

[316] James R. Beck, Dorothy Carey, op. cit., p. 136.

nism held by the Methodists seemed to him to strike at the roots of belief in the grace of God."[317]

Hyper-Calvinism[318] is the opinion that the Calvinist doctrine of Predestination refutes missions, because God would save those He wished without human aid, so that the Great Commission is already fulfilled. Although not typical of Calvinism, this viewpoint was popular, particularly among the Particular Baptists Carey knew.[319]

Carey's significance lies therefore in his harmonization of the Calvinist doctrine of soteriology, learned from Calvin and the Reformed Protestants of the first and second generation, with the call to missions. His precursor, according to Walker,[320] was his friend, Andrew Fuller, who had been a Hyper-Calvinist, but had reconsidered his position and, in his printed sermon, "The Nature of Importance of Walking by Faith" of 1784 and in his book, *The Gospel Worthy of All Acception*, derived the responsibility for missions from the doctrine of predestination itself.[321] Robert Hall's pamphlet, "Help to Zion's Travelers" of 1781, which deeply influenced Carey,[322] also marks the transition from Hyper-Calvinism to missionary Calvinism.[323] In short, "Anglican and Baptist pastors such as Thomas Scott, Andrew Fuller, Robert Hall Sr. and John Sutcliffe ... "[324] aided Carey in overcoming Hyper-Calvinism without surrendering the Calvinist view of salvation. A. Christopher Smith adds, "A neo-Puritan theology much indebted to Jonathan Edwards thus was mediated to Carey without his having to pore over theological tomes."[325]

This demonstrates that not only Carey advocated Calvinist soteriology (and Reformed Postmillennialism), but that the leaders of his British mission society, Andrew Fuller,[326] John Ryland[327] and Thomas Scott, did that

---

[317] Frank Deauville Walker, *William Carey*, op. cit., p. 37.
[318] Cf. Iain H. Murray, *Spurgeon & Hyper-Calvinism: The Battle for Gospel Preaching* (Edinburgh: Banner of Truth Trust, 1995); Kenneth G. Talbot, W. Gary Crampton, *Calvinism, Hyper-Calvinism and Arminianism* (St. Edmonton, Canada: Still Waters Revival Books & Lakeland, Flor.: Whitefield Publ., 1990).
[319] Mary Drewery, *William Carey*, op. cit., p. 31.
[320] Frank Deauville Walker, *William Carey*, op. cit., p. 52-53; See also Ernest A. Payne, "Introduction", op. cit., p. xiii.
[321] Ibid., and James R. Beck, *Dorothy Carey*, op. cit., p. 42.
[322] Mary Drewery, *William Carey*, (with quote by Carey, p. 42); and James R. Beck, *Dorothy Carey*, op. cit., pp. 54-55.
[323] Ibid., p. 54-55.
[324] A. Christopher Smith, "William Carey", op. cit., p. 247.
[325] Ibid.
[326] See Iain Murray, *The Puritan Hope*, op. cit., pp. 139, 146.

as well. Scott wrote "The History of the Synod of Dort" and a history of the origin of the five points of Calvinism. Carey used these works in India and thanked Scott for them expressly.[328]

The same is true of Carey's colleagues in India. This is according to their 'Form of Agreement' of 1805, which gave them a common basis:[329] "we are sure that only those who are ordained to eternal life will believe, and that God alone can add to the church such as shall be saved."[330]

Election and Responsibility

Calvin's doctrine of predestination never denied human responsibility towards divine commandments, including the Great Commandment.[331] Calvin was, after all, the first and perhaps the only Reformer to enjoin world missions. In 1556, he sent two missionaries to Brazil,[332] although the mission was destined to fail. In contrast to Luther, Calvin and Zwingli believed the dissemination of the Gospel to still be under way.[333]

In 1995, Maurus Galm demonstrated that modern Protestant missions began in the Netherlands, where Calvinist theologians were inspired by the missionary efforts of the Catholic Church.[334] Gisbert Voetius[335] discovered

---

[327] Ibid. p. 145-146.
[328] Ibid. p. 145.
[329] Aalbertinus Hermen Oussoren, *William Carey, Especially his Missionary Principles*, op. cit., pp. 274-284, reproduces the text. See Iain Murray's comments in *The Puritan Hope*, op. cit., p. 145.
[330] Iain Murray, *The Puritan Hope*, op. cit., p. 145.
[331] See Paul Jacobs, *Prädestination und Verantwortlichkeit bei Calvin* (Kassel, Germany: J. G. Oncken, 1937). For a modern Calvinist call for missions, see James I. Packer, *Prädestination und Verantwortung*, Neue Studienreihe 5 (Wuppertal, Germany: Brockhaus, 1964) [English title: *Evangelism and the Sovereignty of God*].
[332] Henry R. Van Til, *The Calvinistic Concept of Culture* (Grand Rapids, Mich.: Baker Book House, 1959) p. 93; Louis Igou Hodges, *Reformed Theology Today* (Columbus, GA: Brentwood Christian Press, 1995) pp. 101-104.
[333] Gustav Warneck, *Abriß einer Geschichte der protestantischen Missionen von der Reformation bis auf die Gegenwart*, op. cit., pp. 16, 19.
[334] Maurus Galm, *Das Erwachen des Missionsgedankens im Protestantismus der Niederlande* (München: Franz Xaver Seitz and St. Ottilien: Missionsverlag St. Ottilien, 1915). See the restrictions in A. Goslinga, "Die Anfänge der Mission in Holland", *Allgemeine Missions-Zeitschrift* 49 (1922) pp. 56,63,79-85.
[335] Jürgen Moltmann, "Voetius, Gisbert", *Religion in Geschichte und Gegenwart* Vol 3, ed. Kurt Galling (Tübingen, Germany: J. C. B. Mohr, 1986); Wilhelm Goeters, *Die Vorbereitung des Pietismus in der reformierten Kirche der Niederlande bis zur labadistischen Krise 1670* (Leipzig: 1911) pp. 80-134; Ernst Bizer, "Die re-

the connection between Reformed orthodoxy and the missionary orientation of Reformed Pietism[336] and wrote a thorough missionary theology.[337]

Gisbert Voetius (1589-1676), Professor of Theology and Oriental Languages in Utrecht, Netherlands 1634-1676, was an active member of the Synod of Dordt (1617/19) and a chief proponent of Calvinistic orthodoxy and the most influential Dutch theologian of the 17th century. At the same time, he was one of the spokesmen of the emerging mission oriented Reformed Pietism in the Netherlands and had personal contacts to the English Puritans. His book 'Disputations on Atheism' (1639) and other books against the philosophies of his time show him to be an evangelist to the well educated. Voetius is also the founder of the comparative study of religions for missionary purposes. Nearly all his books and tracts contain long sections on missions, which do not appeal and call to mission work but discuss all major problems of missions scientifically as a fourth part of Systematic Theology 'Theologica elenctica' beside Exegetical, Dogmatic and Practical Theology. Thus Voetius designed the first comprehensive mission theology written by a Protestant. He was well-read in Catholic mission literature. Following a distinction made in Reformed ethics, Voetius combines double predestination as God's absolute will with the conviction that God's moral will is world missions under Biblical promises.

The strict Calvinist, Dutch theologian Adrian Saravia (1531-1613), pastor in Antwerp and Brussels, as well as professor in Leyden (1582-1587), finally Dean in Westminster, was, according to Norman E. Thomas, the only Reformer who fully abandoned the view that the Great Commission had already been fulfilled by the apostles, though Saravia was obviously

---

formierte Orthodoxie und der Cartesianismus", *Zeitschrift für Theologie und Kirche* 55 (1958) pp. 306-372, on Voetius' book 'Disputationen über den Atheismus' (1639) (Bibliographical information p. 308, note 2).

[336] Jürgen Moltmann, "Voetius, Gisbert", op. cit., Col. 1432.

[337] On Voetius' missiology, see: Jan. A. B. Jongeneel, "Voetius' zendingstheologie, de eerste comprehensieve protestantse zendingstheologie", *De onbekende Voetius*, ed. J. van Oort et. al (Kampen, Netherlands: J. H. Kok, 1989) pp. 117-147; H. A. van Andel, *De zendingsleer van Gisbertus Voetius, De onbekende Voetius* (Kampen, Netherlands: J. H. Kok, 1912). On Voetius' theology in general, see: J. van Oort, ed., *De onbekende Voetius*, (Kampen, Netherlands: J. H. Kok, 1989); Ernst Bizer, "Die reformierte Orthodoxie und der Cartesaianismus", *Zeitschrift für Theologie und Kirche* 55 (1958) pp. 306-372. Wilhelm Goeters, *Die Vorbereitung des Pietismus in der reformierten Kirche der Niederlande bis zur labadistischen Krise 1670*, op. cit., pp.80-134.

following in the theological footsteps of Calvin.[338] He had, however, forerunners of importance, such as the Church Father, Aurelius Augustine, who was also the precursor of the Calvinist soteriological view of double Predestination.

Augustine, Aurelius (354-430), bishop of Hippo (North Africa), called the theologian of grace, is the most important theologian of the Roman Catholic Church and spiritual father of all major Reformers, especially Luther, Zwingli and Calvin. In most of his writings Augustine discusses problems of missions,[339] as he was heavily involved in reaching heathen African tribal people and heathen Roman citizens. Gonsalvus Walter has combined those quotations to a full-orbed theology of missions.[340] Augustine reconciled the belief in double predestination with an urgent call, that it is the will of God to preach the Gospel everywhere. In his famous Letter No. 199,[341] Augustine denies that the Great Commission was already achieved by the apostles because, exegetically, the commission goes "till the end of the world" and practically, he knows of "innumerable barbarian tribes in Africa to whom the gospel has not yet been preached."[342] God had not promised not only the Romans to Abraham but all nations. Before the return of Jesus Christ the majority of nations and people will become Christians.[343] This is a typical postmillennial[344] viewpoint.

Chaney has emphasized that modern Protestant world missions began with two Calvinist groups: the chaplains of the Dutch East India Company and with the Puritans, who tried to reach the Indians of North America.[345]

Carey could already read Dutch well before writing the "Enquiry" and had translated two works which demonstrated missionary Calvinism.[346]

---

[338] Norman E. Thomas ed., *Classic Texts in Mission and World Christianity*, op. cit., pp. 41-43.

[339] Gerhard Metzger, *Kirche und Mission in den Briefen Augustins*, Allgemeine Mission-Studien 20 (Gütersloh, Germany: C. Bertelsmann, 1936); and F. van der Meer, *Augustinus der Seelsorger* (Cologne: J. P. Bachem, 1958).

[340] P. Gonsalvus Walter O. M. Cap., *Die Heidenmission nach der Lehre des heiligen Augustinus*, Missionswissenschaftliche Abhandlungen und Texte 3 (Münster, Germany: Aschendorff, 1921).

[341] Maurice Wiles and Mark Santer ed., *Documents in Early Christian Thought* (Cambridge: Cambridge University Press, 1975) pp. 259-264); Norman E. Thomas ed., *Classic Texts in Mission and World Christianity*, op. cit., p. 18.

[342] Ibid. (both editions), Letter 199, Part 46.

[343] Ibid. (both editions), Letter 199, Part 47-49.

[344] This is the judgment of Millard J. Erickson, *Christian Theology*, op. cit., p. 1206.

[345] Charles L. Chaney, *The Birth of Missions in America*, op. cit., p. ix.

[346] Ernest A. Payne, "Two Dutch Translations by Carey: An Angus Library Find", op. cit. Payne's object is to refute the criticism that Carey's knowledge of so many

Of all of Carey's precursors who denied the complete fulfillment of the Great Commission by the apostles, the most important was Augustine Aurelius,[347] whose theology already leaned toward Postmillennialism, and who is considered the father of Calvinist soteriology.

> "Augustine predates by more than fifteen centuries William Carey's analysis, that the apostles did not complete the Lord's Great Commission to 'go into all the world'."[348]

Tom Nettles has, for example, shown that almost all eighteenth century Baptist theologians and mission leaders taught a Calvinist soteriology.[349]

The reason for the almost exclusively Reformed nature of Protestant world missions from the sixteenth to the eighteenth centuries was the rise of the Netherlands (The East Indian Trading Company was founded in 1602) and England as sea powers;[350] two Protestant countries, whose churches had Reformed Confessions.[351]

Calvinism in the "Enquiry"

Carey derives the very possibility and the responsibility for missions from the doctrine of providence itself, while Hyper-Calvinism derived its belief from the doctrine of predestination, stating that the heathen were lost unless God brought them the Gospel without human assistance. 'Providence' in Calvinist theology describes God's sovereignty. Carey uses this term six times in the "Enquiry"[352] and often in other writings[353] as well. As a Cal-

---

languages could have been only superficial, his translations are sound. James Beck, *Dorothy, Carey,* op. cit., p. 53, supports this view.
[347] Norman E. Thomas ed., *Classic Texts in Mission and World Christianity,* op. cit., pp. 17-20. On page 18, Thomas quotes Augustine, " ... that the Lord's coming will take place when the whole world is filled with the gospel."
[348] Ibid., p. 17.
[349] Tom Nettles "Missionary Theology of the Early Southern Baptists", *Reformation Today* (1985), pp. 9-22.
[350] Gustav Warneck, *Abriß einer Geschichte der protestantischen Missionen von der Reformation bis auf die Gegenwart,* op. cit., p. 39.
[351] Philip E. Hughes, "Thirty-nine Articles", *Encyclopedia of the Reformed Faith,* ed. Donald K. McKim, op. cit., p. 369. Hughes demonstrates that not only the Puritans, but also the Anglican Church was Reformed. The Thirty-nine Articles are Reformed in their view of the Scriptures, of salvation and of the sacraments. The standard commentary on the Thirty-nine Articles is W. H. Griffith Thomas, *The Principles of Theology: An Introduction to the Thirty-Nine Articles* (1930, repr. London: Vine Books, 1978) pp. xxxiii, xlix.
[352] Carey, "Enquiry," op. cit., pp. 11, 67, 68, 80.

vinist Baptist, he believed in Providence unreservedly and continually based his belief in the necessity of missions on this idea.

> "It has been said that we ought not to force our way, but to wait for the openings, and leadings of Providence; but it might with equal propriety be answered in this case, neither ought we to neglect embracing those openings in providence which daily present themselves to us. What openings of providence do we wait for? ... Where a command exists nothing can be necessary to render it binding but a removal of those obstacles which render obedience impossible, and these are removed already. Natural impossibility can never be pleaded so long as facts exist to prove the contrary."[354]

Even later, Carey never changed his view. James Beck adds,

> "Carey never strayed far from his Calvinistic roots when reflecting on his God of providence. God was a God of order and control."[355]

As we have already seen, in the "Enquiry" Carey distinguishes between God's sovereign will, Providence, and God's moral will, the basis for human duty. Not only here does he prove himself to be a pupil of Calvinist ethics. His arguments, for example, distinguish between the moral and the ceremonial law,[356] and discuss the question, what factors revoke a Biblical commandment, with reasoning typical to Reformed ethics.[357] In the churches he served prior to his departure for India, he exercised a strict church discipline typical of Calvinism,[358] and followed Puritan ethics in many minor decisions, such as journeys on Sundays.[359]

Carey's Struggles for Social Change

Carey's involvement in the battle against social injustice[360] was also an element of his missionary work and was evident in the "Enquiry" through the texts cited above on religious freedom and the slave trade. These en-

---

[353] See the citations in James R. Beck, *Dorothy Carey*, op. cit., pp. 44, 45, 54, 184.
[354] Carey, "Enquiry," op. cit., pp. 10-11.
[355] James R. Beck, *Dorothy Carey*, op. cit., p. 184.
[356] Carey, "Enquiry," op. cit., p. 9-10.
[357] Carey, "Enquiry," op. cit., p. 9-10.
[358] Harald Schilling, "Der geistige Werdegang William Careys ... ", op. cit., p.88.
[359] James R. Beck, *Dorothy Carey*, op. cit., p. 87.
[360] Ibid., p. 136,170-172; E. Walroth, "William Carey," *Allgemeine Missions-Zeitschrift* 14 (1887), pp. 97-123 (Particulary the article, "Careys Verdienste um Literatur und Humanität"); G. Schott, *William Carey, der Vater der gegenwärtigen Missionsbewegung*, op. cit., pp. 24-27.

deavors point to his Calvinist background, which considers possible the Christianization of a nation in ethical and in social-political concerns.[361] Carey ate no sugar in England, since it was produced by slaves, and prayed throughout his entire life for the emancipation of slaves.[362] Shortly after his arrival in 1802, he began an investigation on the commission of the governor into religious killings in Hindu India, and soon attained the prohibition of the ritual killing of children – babies were annually thrown into the Ganges once a year on the Island of Saugor.[363] After a lifelong battle, in 1826 he was able to obtain the prohibition of *sati*, the incineration of widows.[364] Both prohibitions were by and large successful.

Carey was just as outspoken in his opinions on slavery[365] and the caste system, which he in no case wanted to allow within the Church, even at the cost of advantages for his missionary efforts.[366] In this point, he differed from the Halle-Danish mission and the Society for the Propagation of Christian Knowledge (SPCK), which retained the caste system even in the

---

[361] Aalbertinus Hermen Oussoren, *William Carey, Especially His Missionary Principles*, op. cit., pp. 189-190.

[362] Bruce J. Nichols, "The Theology of William Carey". op. cit., pp. 121-122 proved, that this was founded in Carey's theology as was the case with all his engagement in social affairs.

[363] E. Daniels Potts, *British Baptist Missionaries in India 1793-1837*, op. cit., pp. 141-144; Frank Deauville Walker, *William Carey*, op. cit., pp. 197-199; Basil Miller, *William Carey*, op. cit., p. 93.

[364] The most detailed study can be found in E. Daniel Potts, *British Baptist Missionaries in India 1793-1837*, op. cit., pp. 144-157. Texts by Carey are printed in Pearce Carey, *William Carey*, op. cit., pp. 170-173. Cf. Brian Stanley, *The History of the Baptist Missionary Society 1792-1992*, op. cit., p. 44-45; A. Schillbach, "William Carey als Bahnbrecher der evangelischen Mission", op. cit., pp. 181-182; Frank Deauville Walker, *William Carey*, op. cit., pp. 199-201; Basil Miller, *William Carey*, op. cit., pp. 137-138; Kellsye Finnie, *William Carey*, op. cit., pp. 141-143; James R. Beck, *Dorothy Carey*, op. cit., 170-171; G. Schott, *William Carey, der Vater der gegenwärtigen Missionsbewegung*, op. cit., pp. 27-30.

[365] Aalbertinus Hermen Oussoren, *William Carey, Especially His Missionary Principles*, op. cit., pp. 159-160; E. Daniel Potts, *British Baptist Missionaries in India 1793-1837*, op. cit., pp. 191-193.

[366] E. Daniel Potts, *British Baptist Missionaries in India 1793-1837*, op. cit., pp. 158-159;. Aalbertinus Hermen Oussoren, *William Carey, Especially His Missionary Principles*, op. cit., p. 195; Kellsye Finnie, *William Carey*, op. cit., p. 109; James R. Beck, *Dorothy Carey*, op. cit., p. 135-136; Mary Drewery, *William Carey*, pp. 104-105; A. Christopher Smith, "Myth and Missiology: A Methodological Approach to Pre-Victorian Mission of the Serampore Trio", *International Review of Mission* 83 (1994) pp. 451-475, pp. 461-463.

Lord's Supper. Carey insisted that the convert break with the system before being baptized.[367] He wrote,

> "Perhaps this is one of the greatest barriers to conversion with which the devil ever bound the children of men. This is my comfort, that God can break it."[368]

In this he was in harmony with his fellow workers. So Ward insisted that missionaries would dig the graves for missionaries and other Europeans. Thus, they did a job which was even forbidden for members of the lowest casts.[369]

Carey's achievements in translating the Scripture[370] and in preserving[371] Indian languages,[372] particularly his grammars,[373] are uncontested.[374] He

---

[367] Ruth Rouse, "William Carey's Pleasing Dream," *International Review of Missions* 38 ((1949) pp. 181-192. Graham Houghton, "Caste in the Protestant Churches: An Historical Perspective", *Evangelical Review of Theology* 12 (1988) 4, pp. 325-343 discusses the handling of the caste system by missionaries in India. See also *The India Church Growth Quarterly* 7 (1985) 2. Cf. for the modern situation *Gerechtigkeit für die Unberührbaren: Beiträge zur indischen Dalit-Theologie*, Weltmission heute no. 15 (Hamburg: EMW, 1997²).

[368] William Carey's diary, quoted in Mary Drewery, *William Carey*, p. 79.

[369] According to S. Pearce Carey, *William Carey*, op. cit., pp. 223.

[370] Aalbertinus Hermen Oussoren, *William Carey, Especially His Missionary Principles*, op. cit., p. 118, note 1, provides a table of the translations in the various languges with dates of appearance. James R. Beck, *Dorothy Carey*. op. cit., pp. 168-170 mentions six Bibles, 23 New Testaments and 10 parts as Carey's own achievements. Mary Drewery, *William Carey*, op.cit., pp. 155-158,192 lists six complete Bibles and 29 parts as Carey's work. In cooperation with his team, he also completed 19 Bibles and 17 parts. See also Frank Deauville Walker, *William Carey*, op. cit., pp. 219-232; S. Pearce Carey, *William Carey*, op. cit., pp. 385-394.

[371] See as example from a speaker of those languages Ramesh Khatry, "William Carey – The First Publisher in Nepali", *Dharma Deepika: A South Asian Journal of Missiological Research* 3 (1999) pp. 41-44.

[372] E. Daniel Potts, *British Baptist Missionaries in India 1793-1837*, op. cit., pp. 79-113 provides the most thorough information. See also E. Wallroth, "William Carey", *Allgemeine Missions-Zeitschrift* 14 (1887) pp. 97-123. On pages 114-116, the author lists the translations in "Careys Verdienste um Literatur und Humanität."

[373] Johann Schmidt, "Carlotte Emilia von Rumohr und William Carey," op. cit., p. 45 mentions particularly the Marathi Grammar of 1805, the Sanskrit Grammar of 1806, the Punjabi Grammar of 1817, the Karnatak Grammar of 1817, the Benali Grammar of 1818 and the Bengali Dictionary in 8 Volumes 1818-1830.

[374] E. Daniel Potts, *British Baptist Missionaries in India 1793-1837*, op. cit., pp. 81-89 provides a modern discussion of the value of Carey's Bible translations. Potts also discusses the value of his grammars and the work on Bengali texts on pages 79-113, and describes the recognition of Carey's efforts to preserve Bengali and

aided in doubling the number of Bible translations in the eighteenth century from thirty to nearly sixty, and played a major role in keeping these languages from dying out, by making them written languages.

The team founded forty-five free schools[375] with about 10,000 pupils[376] of all social classes, the still extant Serampore College[377] and several newspapers in English and in native languages to further the education of the Indian people. Serampore College, modeled on the universities of Copenhagen and Kiel,[378] was India's first university.

Finally, through the Agricultural Society of India, founded in 1820,[379] he did much to improve India's farming system. E. Daniel Potts writes, "Those who follow Colin Clark's lead in thinking that contributions to the development of India would ultimately be of far greater benefit than hand-to-mouth poor relief will applaud the advanced thinking of William Carey."[380]

In 1993, many Indian linguists, scientists and historians as well as theologians gathered for a jubilee symposium, emphasizing the great achievements of Carey for all branches of Indian society.[381]

Carey and his colleagues were, however, no instruments of the colonial government. Their activities "led them to cooperate or, more often, conflict with the constituted authorities."[382]

---

his publications of Bengali texts in books and journals. In 1830, William Greenfield, the renowned linguist of Cambridge University, defended Carey's translation efforts. See William Greenfield, *A Defence of the Serampore Mahratta Version of the New Testament*, London, 1830.

[375] E. Daniel Potts, *British Baptist Missionaries in India 1793-1837*, op. cit., pp. 115-129. See also G. Schott, *William Carey, der Vater der gegenwärtigen Missionsbewegung*, op. cit., pp. 34-35.

[376] A. Schillbach, "William Carey: Eine Jubiläumserinnerung," op. cit., p. 49.

[377] E. Daniel Potts, *British Baptist Missionaries in India 1793-1837*, op. cit., pp. 129-136 on the college's early history.

[378] Johann Schmidt, "Carlotte Emilia von Rumohr und William Carey," op. cit., p. 49. Cf. for the theological faculty A. Christopher Smith, "Myth and Missiology: A Methodological Approach to Pre-Victorian Mission of the Serampore Trio", op.cit., pp. 458-460. According to p. 460, this faculty lost all importance after Carey and the Serampore-Trio.

[379] G. Schott, *William Carey, der Vater der gegenwärtigen Missionsbewegung*, op. cit., pp. 30-34; E. Daniel Potts, *British Baptist Missionaries in India 1793-1837*, op. cit., pp. 70-75.

[380] Ibid, p. 70-71.

[381] J. T. K. Daniel, Roger E. Hedlund ed., *Carey's Obligation and Indian Renaissance* (Serampore, India: Council of Serampore College, 1993)

[382] Ibid., pp. 169-204 describes the relationship to the colonial government in detail.

The "Enquiry" shows how Carey argued for native leadership,[383] which aroused criticism not only in politics, but also in the church. In 1834, fifty missionaries (Six Europeans, Anglo-Indians and Indians) were working in Serampore with Carey's team of nineteen.[384] The British General Baptists, in particular, criticized the Particular Baptists' preference for native workers, which hindered many good British missionaries from working in Serampore.[385] Carey plead for the 'modern' principle that the missionary should be able to make decisions independent of their mission boards,[386] which led to the most difficult crisis of the Serampore mission station and to a temporary dissolution of the ties between the station and the mission board.[387]

4. Carey's Statistics

The significance of the statistic survey in the "Enquiry" is usually ignored, although the statistics and the geographical material take up most of the book.[388] W. Bieder writes, "Carey challenged Christianity to accept its responsibility to become familiar with the world's religious condition. No missions without sufficient information! With astonishing accuracy, Carey drew up a sound statistic on world religion, thus recognizing the importance of statistics for mission activity."[389] The first German edition identified the geographical data necessary to evaluating Carey's information and his graphs.[390]

---

[383] See Brian Stanley, *The History of the Baptist Missionary Society 1792-1992*, op. cit., pp. 47-57 ("The Planting of a National Church"), sees the planting of indigenous churches under indigenenous leadership as the second pillar beside the belief in the sovereignty of God (pp. 36-47), on which the work of the Serampore-Trio rested.

[384] E. Daniel Potts, *British Baptist Missionaries in India 1793-1837*, op. cit., p. 33.

[385] Ibid. p. 34.

[386] Basil Miller, *William Carey*, op. cit., pp. 62,128-130; Mary Drewery, *William Carey*, op. cit., pp. 170-171. Joshua Marshmann explains the situation in *Thoughts on Missions to India* (Serampore: 1825).

[387] A. Christopher Smith, "The Edinburgh Connection: Between the Serampore Mission and Western Missiology", op. cit., pp. 185-209; Brian Stanley, *The History of the Baptist Missionary Society 1792-1992*, op. cit., pp. 57-67.

[388] An exception is Jim Montgomery, *Eine ganze Nation gewinnen: Die DAWN-Strategie* (Lörrach: Wolfgang Simson Verlag, 1990), pp. 101-103; engl. Original: 7 Million Churches To Go. William Carey Library: Pasadena (CA), 1979

[389] W. Bieder, "William Carey 1761-1834," op. cit. p. 161.

[390] William Carey, *Eine Untersuchung über die Verpflichtung der Christen, Mittel einzusetzen für die Bekehrung der Heiden*, edition afem – mission classics 1, ed.

Almost every new beginning in missions has been accompanied by statistical achievements, for statistics serve as the basis for prayer and orientation. Carey's statistics, as well as those of Theodor Christlieb[391] (1879) and Patrick Johnstone's *Operation World*[392] have been and still are excellent reference material for 'secular' interests, and it is no accident that Carey's knowledge was almost unrivaled in his time, just as the ethnologists of Wycliffe Bible Translators know more than others about the languages of the present. His suggestion of 1806,[393] that an international missions conference be held in 1810 in Cape Town, South Africa, was the logical result, even though it was not realized for a century in Edinburgh.

---

and translated by Klaus Fiedler and Thomas Schirrmacher (Bonn: Verlag für Kultur und Wissenschaft, 1993).

[391] Thomas Schirrmacher, *Theodor Christlieb und seine Missionstheologie*, op. cit., pp. 171-172. Christlieb's survey of the mission situation in all parts of the earth, 'Der gegenwärtige Stand der Heidenmission: Eine Weltüberschau' ('Protestant Missions to the Heathen', 1880) was printed in several revised editions in German, and in several English editions in London, New York and Calcutta. It was also translated into French, Danish and Swedish.

[392] Patrick Johnstone, *Operation World*, several editions since 1978. James Beck, *Dorothy Carey*, op. cit., p. 63, also compares Carey with Johnstone.

[393] Ruth Rouse, "William Carey's Pleasing Dream," op. cit., pp. 181-192.

World Evangelical Alliance

World Evangelical Alliance is a global ministry working with local churches around the world to join in common concern to live and proclaim the Good News of Jesus in their communities. WEA is a network of churches in 129 nations that have each formed an evangelical alliance and over 100 international organizations joining together to give a worldwide identity, voice and platform to more than 600 million evangelical Christians. Seeking holiness, justice and renewal at every level of society – individual, family, community and culture, God is glorified and the nations of the earth are forever transformed.

Christians from ten countries met in London in 1846 for the purpose of launching, in their own words, "a new thing in church history, a definite organization for the expression of unity amongst Christian individuals belonging to different churches." This was the beginning of a vision that was fulfilled in 1951 when believers from 21 countries officially formed the World Evangelical Fellowship. Today, 150 years after the London gathering, WEA is a dynamic global structure for unity and action that embraces 600 million evangelicals in 129 countries. It is a unity based on the historic Christian faith expressed in the evangelical tradition. And it looks to the future with vision to accomplish God's purposes in discipling the nations for Jesus Christ.

Commissions:

- Theology
- Missions
- Religious Liberty
- Women's Concerns
- Youth
- Information Technology

Initiatives and Activities

- Ambassador for Human Rights
- Ambassador for Refugees
- Creation Care Task Force
- Global Generosity Network
- International Institute for Religious Freedom
- International Institute for Islamic Studies
- Leadership Institute
- Micah Challenge
- Global Human Trafficking Task Force
- Peace and Reconciliation Initiative
- UN-Team

Church Street Station
P.O. Box 3402
New York, NY 10008-3402
Phone +[1] 212 233 3046
Fax +[1] 646-957-9218
www.worldea.org

Giving Hands

GIVING HANDS GERMANY (GH) was established in 1995 and is officially recognized as a nonprofit foreign aid organization. It is an international operating charity that – up to now – has been supporting projects in about 40 countries on four continents. In particular we care for orphans and street children. Our major focus is on Africa and Central America. GIVING HANDS always mainly provides assistance for self-help and furthers human rights thinking.

The charity itself is not bound to any church, but on the spot we are cooperating with churches of all denominations. Naturally we also cooperate with other charities as well as governmental organizations to provide assistance as effective as possible under the given circumstances.

The work of GIVING HANDS GERMANY is controlled by a supervisory board. Members of this board are Manfred Feldmann, Colonel V. Doner and Kathleen McCall. Dr. Christine Schirrmacher is registered as legal manager of GIVING HANDS at the local district court. The local office and work of the charity are coordinated by Rev. Horst J. Kreie as executive manager. Dr. theol. Thomas Schirrmacher serves as a special consultant for all projects.

Thanks to our international contacts companies and organizations from many countries time and again provide containers with gifts in kind which we send to the different destinations where these goods help to satisfy elementary needs. This statutory purpose is put into practice by granting nutrition, clothing, education, construction and maintenance of training centers at home and abroad, construction of wells and operation of water treatment systems, guidance for self-help and transportation of goods and gifts to areas and countries where needy people live.

GIVING HANDS has a publishing arm under the leadership of Titus Vogt, that publishes human rights and other books in English, Spanish, Swahili and other languages.

These aims are aspired to the glory of the Lord according to the basic Christian principles put down in the Holy Bible.

Baumschulallee 3a • D-53115 Bonn • Germany
Phone: +49 / 228 / 695531 • Fax +49 / 228 / 695532
www.gebende-haende.de • info@gebende-haende.de

Martin Bucer Seminary

Faithful to biblical truth
Cooperating with the Evangelical Alliance
Reformed

Solid training for the Kingdom of God
- Alternative theological education
- Study while serving a church or working another job
- Enables students to remain in their own churches
- Encourages independent thinking
- Learning from the growth of the universal church.

Academic
- For the Bachelor's degree: 180 Bologna-Credits
- For the Master's degree: 120 additional Credits
- Both old and new teaching methods: All day seminars, independent study, term papers, etc.

Our Orientation:
- Complete trust in the reliability of the Bible
- Building on reformation theology
- Based on the confession of the German Evangelical Alliance
- Open for innovations in the Kingdom of God

Our Emphasis:
- The Bible
- Ethics and Basic Theology
- Missions
- The Church

Our Style:
- Innovative
- Relevant to society
- International
- Research oriented
- Interdisciplinary

Structure
- 15 study centers in 7 countries with local partners
- 5 research institutes
- President: Prof. Dr. Thomas Schirrmacher
  Vice President: Prof. Dr. Thomas K. Johnson
- Deans: Thomas Kinker, Th.D.;
  Titus Vogt, lic. theol., Carsten Friedrich, M.Th.

Missions through research
- Institute for Religious Freedom
- Institute for Islamic Studies
- Institute for Life and Family Studies
- Institute for Crisis, Dying, and Grief Counseling
- Institute for Pastoral Care

www.bucer.eu • info@bucer.eu
Berlin I Bielefeld I Bonn I Chemnitz I Hamburg I Munich I Pforzheim
Innsbruck I Istanbul I Izmir I Linz I Prague I São Paulo I Tirana I Zurich

www.ingramcontent.com/pod-product-compliance
Lightning Source LLC
Chambersburg PA
CBHW050825160426
43192CB00010B/1902